On Wings of Freedom

The Hillel Haggadah for the Nights of Passover

On Wings of Freedom

The Hillel Haggadah for the Nights of Passover

Edited and translated by
Rabbi Richard N. Levy

B'nai B'rith Hillel Foundations
in association with
Ktav Publishing House, Inc.
Hoboken, NJ
1989

ISBN 0-88125-319-7

Manufactured in the United States of America

INTRODUCTION

On Bringing Forth a People—
And Its Truth

Tradition tells us that when Moses wrote down the words of
Torah which God was dictating to him, he wrote merely chapter
headings (*rashei perakim*), leaving it to subsequent generations
of students and scholars to "fill in" the chapters through their
questions and reflections on the written text. Each word, each letter, of the Written Torah is to be considered a chapter heading,
pregnant with interpretations which it is the responsibility of
every serious student of Torah to bring to birth.

The Passover Haggadah is an example of one such birth. Its
basic outline is included in the Mishnah (a law code completed by
the second century C.E.), and it is a dramatic commentary on but
one verse of the story: "You shall tell your child in that day,
saying, 'It is because of what Adonai did for me when I came forth
out of Egypt'" (Exodus 13:8).

Why is telling the story so important? Perhaps because each
time we tell the story, we are reliving the Exodus, literally reliving it—living another dimension of it, experiencing parts we
missed in earlier years, bringing to light truths that our own times
have revealed to us, preparing the ground for new understandings
that subsequent generations will bring forth. "Bring forth"—that
is what "Exodus" means: God brought us forth from Egypt as a
newly-birthed people. By bringing forth new insight from an
opaque text, we perpetuate God's work with our own.

Giving birth to truth, bringing it from darkness into light, is
not for us an intellectual exercise. It is an act of love, an act that
reveals the love of God. The Biblical Scroll (*megillah*) which is
read on Passover is Shir Ha-Shirim, the Song of Songs, traditionally understood to be the love song of God and Israel before their
wedding journey across the sea, when God brought us "on wings
of eagles" (Exodus 19:4), on wings of freedom. The Song of
Songs enjoins us "not to awaken love before it pleases"—but
Passover is the time of love, the time of the revelation of God's

love for Israel; it is the time when God pleases to awaken us to our calling as the Beloved of the *Kadosh Baruch Hu*, the Blessed Holy One.

This Haggadah, whose chapter headings come from the Song of Songs, is intended to allow those who use it to fill in the chapters through reflections which flow from the directions of a traditional Seder. Many households tend to read the Haggadah straight through, as though afraid to pause lest the participants' hunger overtake them. This Haggadah believes, with the prophet Amos (8:11), that our real hunger is for the word of God, and that if the Seder can satisfy some of that hunger, the Passover meal will not only nurture the body, but the soul as well.

Features of This Haggadah

To that end, almost every section of this Haggadah features a triad of Directions, Questions, and Reflections.

1) *Directions* clearly identify the appropriate actions to be taken in each section of the Haggadah.
2) *Questions*, found in the Leader's Edition (along with suggestions for responding to them) encourage both leader and participants to look closely at the Haggadah text and some of its sources to understand better some of the underlying issues of the Seder as well as reflect on the participants' own experiences of it.
3) *Reflections* include optional readings or brief interpretations relating to portions of the Haggadah. Some reflections also attempt to describe the meaning of such often-ignored details as covering and uncovering the matzah, and raising and lowering the wine cup. These ritual gestures, along with the breaking and hiding of the matzah, are part of the silent drama of matzah and wine which undergirds this meal of transformation. As the evening progresses, the matzah of affliction is changed into the bread of freedom, while the wine, representing God's holy presence, remains steadfast throughout both affliction and redemption.

This Haggadah is intended to be used at Hillel Foundations around the country, as well as other community Seders and private homes. It contains essentially the entire traditional text as well as alternative readings in almost every major section. Since women as well as men were redeemed from Egypt, the language of the text is inclusive, with the matriarchs included in parentheses in the Hebrew text.

The wide variety of choices is intended not only to meet the needs of disparate student congregations (as well as other potential users), but to offer the possibility of conducting several very different Sedarim not only on the first two nights of Pesach, but, as is increasingly becoming the custom, on other nights as well. Thus, in addition to alternative readings for most sections, the rite of Sefirat Ha-Omer (Counting the Omer) is included for all the nights of Pesach.

Arranging the Table

The table(s) at which the Seder meal is eaten should be set in a festive manner, with a pillow at the leader's place, and if possible, at others' seats as well. Each participant should have a *cup* which will be filled four times during the meal with grape wine or grape juice. An especially beautiful *Elijah's cup* should be provided, which may be filled by the leader or filled from the participants' cups at the time of the opening of the door (see p. 95).

If guests are to dip their hands during U-re-chatz and Ra-cha-tza, a special table should be provided to which guests can go for handwashing. On the table should be pitchers or cups of water to pour over one's hands, bowls to receive the water, and towels to wipe the hands. It is also possible to put these items on the Seder table and pass them around.

If the reading on page 24, "This is the bread," is to be done, an empty chair should be provided at the table.

In front of the leader stands the Seder plate, on which are placed the following:

1) *Three matzot*, sheets of unleavened bread, separated by cloths which enable the matzah to be covered and uncovered. (Sometimes the matzot are set on a plate of their own.)
2) *Karpas*, the first vegetable dipped in salt water. Parsley or celery are usually used, but a potato or radish can be substituted.

3) A dish of *salt water*, to dip the karpas.
4) Two commemorative dishes which are not eaten: a roasted shankbone, *zeroa*, representing the paschal lamb, and a roasted egg, *betzah*, representing the chagigah, or special festival offering.
5) *Maror*, bitter herbs, for which romaine lettuce (*chazeret*), endive, or horseradish is used. Some Seder plates have room for two kinds of maror, one eaten when the blessing for maror is said, the other when it is eaten as the "Hillel sandwich," *korech*.
6) *Charoset*, a preserve representing bricks and mortar, is prepared of chopped and pounded fruits such as apples, nuts, and almonds, mixed with cinnamon or wine.

If possible, each participant should have a small plate containing karpas, salt water, maror, and charoset. Several plates of matzot and carrot or celery sticks should be within reach of everyone.

Suggestions for the conduct of the Seder will be found in the Leader's Edition.

THE SEARCH FOR CHAMETZ

Reflections

Pesach is a holiday of bringing-out. The historical event of God's bringing Israel out of Egypt is emulated in miniature by the leader bringing the matzah out from its cover, and by a participant (usually a child) bringing the afikomon out of its hiding place.

The idea behind all the bringing-outs is that what we are rescuing should not be where it is. Israel should not have been enslaved in the darkness of Mitzrayim, the Hebrew word for Egypt which literally means "the narrow, confining places."

And yet, Israel went into Egypt originally as part of God's plan: there was a famine in the Near East, and the only place where bread could be obtained was in Egypt. It was appropriate that Israel should have gone into Egypt in Joseph's time, but because Israel was misused, oppressed, there, it was later necessary that we be taken out, lest we lose all sense of our destiny as a people of God.

All during the year we eat leavened bread. We say a blessing over it (*Ha-Motzi*), we use it on Shabbat and holidays and ordinary days.

Clearly there is nothing wrong with these loaves that get all puffed up from the yeast that works mysteriously inside them. It is appropriate to eat this puffed-up grain.

But sometimes we put yeast not only into the bread but in ourselves. We get puffed up too: in pride, in appetite, in lust, in greed. We feel unsatisfied with our own selves, with simple needs. Our appetites lead us to take advantage of others, to seek power over others, to indulge bodily needs without regard to our health, to propriety, to modesty. At such a time, because we have misused the yeasty things in our lives, it is necessary that we take them out of our lives, lest we lose all sense of our destiny as a people of God.

The rabbis say that yeast is like the *yetzer ha-ra*, our animal inclination, which works insidiously inside us to thwart the aims of the *yetzer tov*, our divine inclination. We need our *yetzer ha-ra*—without our bodies, without appetite, without desire, we would not be human, we could not do any mitzvot. The first paragraph of the Shema, the *Ve-a-hav-ta*, urges us to love God *be-chol le-vav-cha*, with all our hearts, which the rabbis understood to mean with both our *yetzer tov* and our *yetzer ha-ra*.

Too often, though, we don't use our *yetzer ha-ra* in the service of God. Therefore, for one week a year, during Pesach, we take out the visible evidence of the *yetzer ha-ra* from our lives by cleaning our homes of leavened foodstuffs, called *chametz*. Before Pesach begins, we scrub shelves, clean refrigerators and ovens, and in the process understand something of the hard labor of the Israelites as we grunt and groan the chametz out of our lives.

When we have gotten rid of every piece of chametz we can find, we save ten pieces (a number with Kabbalistic overtones) and hide them around the house. Shortly before dark on the night before Pesach (or on Thursday evening if Passover occurs on Shabbat), we collect the ten pieces and set them aside till morning. It is customary to use a candle for light while doing so, and to gather the pieces by using a feather to brush them onto a wooden spoon.

We might even try to identify each of the ten pieces with one of the abuses of our *yetzer ha-ra* of which we have been guilty since Yom Kippur, and reflect on them during the night. It is Spring, after all, time for a new start, time for a new flowering of the selves God created us to be.

DIRECTIONS: Before looking for the chametz pieces, armed with candle (or other light source), feather, and spoon, the searchers say:

בָּרוּךְ אַתָּה יְיָ אֱלֹהֵינוּ מֶלֶךְ הָעוֹלָם אֲשֶׁר קִדְּשָׁנוּ
בְּמִצְוֹתָיו וְצִוָּנוּ עַל בִּעוּר חָמֵץ:

Ba-ruch a-ta A-do-nai E-lo-hei-nu me-lech ha-o-lam, a-sher ki-de-sha-nu be-mitz-vo-tav ve-tzi-va-nu al bi-ur cha-metz.

You are praised, Adonai our God, Monarch of time and space, who shares Your holiness with us through Your mitz-vot, and now bestows on us the mitzvah of destroying our chametz.

DIRECTIONS: The search begins, using the candle to probe the corners of our inner lives as deeply as we probe the corners of our homes. After the search, when all chametz not to be used for breakfast the next day has been gathered in a safe place, the searchers say:

כָּל חֲמִירָא וַחֲמִיעָא דְּאִכָּא בִרְשׁוּתִי. דְּלָא חֲמִתֵּה וּדְלָא
בְעַרְתֵּה. לִבְטִיל וְלֶהֱוֵי הֶפְקֵר כְּעַפְרָא דְּאַרְעָא:

Kol cha-mi-ra va-cha-mi-a de-i-ka vir-shu-ti de-la cha-mi-tei u-de-la bi-ar-tei, liv-til ve-le-he-vei hef-ker ke-af-ra de-ar-a.

Every sort of chametz in my possession which has not met my gaze and which I have not destroyed, let it be null and void, ownerless, like the dust of the earth.

Reflection

This is the first transformation wrought for Pesach: chametz has become like the dust of the earth. Soon matzah, beginning the Seder as a symbol of affliction, will be transformed into freedom.

DIRECTIONS: On the morning of Pesach, after the last meal of chametz, leftovers are added to the chametz gathered from the previous night and all are burned, or otherwise removed from the house. Symbolically included in the burning might also be the recollections of the ten abuses of our *yetzer ha-ra* that we enumerated the night before. After the burning, all say:

כָּל חֲמִירָא וַחֲמִיעָא דְּאִכָּא בִרְשׁוּתִי. דַּחֲמִיתֵּהּ וּדְלָא חֲמִתֵּהּ. דְּבִעֲרְתֵּהּ וּדְלָא בִעֲרְתֵּהּ. לִבְטִיל וְלֶהֱוֵי הֶפְקֵר כְּעַפְרָא דְאַרְעָא:

Kol cha-mi-rah va-cha-mi-a de-i-ka vir-shu-ti, da-cha-mi-tei u-de-la cha-mi-tei, de-vi-ar-tei u-de-la vi-ar-tei, liv-til ve-le-he-vei hef-ker ke-af-ra de-ar-a.

Every sort of chametz in my possession, which has met my gaze or has not met my gaze, which I have destroyed or have not destroyed, let it be null and void, ownerless, like the dust of the earth.

יְהִי רָצוֹן מִלְּפָנֶיךָ יְיָ אֱלֹהֵינוּ וֵאלֹהֵי אֲבוֹתֵינוּ (וְאִמּוֹתֵינוּ) שֶׁכְּשֵׁם שֶׁאֲנִי מְבַעֵר (מְבַעֶרֶת) חָמֵץ מִבֵּיתִי וּמֵרְשׁוּתִי כָּךְ תְּבַעֵר אֶת יִצְרֵנוּ הָרָע מֵאִתָּנוּ וְתִתֶּן לָנוּ לֵב בָּשָׂר. וְכָל הָרִשְׁעָה כְּעָשָׁן תִּכְלֶה וְתַעֲבִיר מֶמְשֶׁלֶת זָדוֹן מִן הָאָרֶץ. וְטַהֵר לִבֵּנוּ לְעָבְדְּךָ בֶּאֱמֶת וְיַחֵד לְבָבֵנוּ לְאַהֲבָה וּלְיִרְאָה אֶת שְׁמֶךָ:

May it be Your will, Adonai, God of our fathers and mothers, that as I have destroyed chametz from my home and from my possessions, so may You help me destroy the power of the *yetzer ha-ra* over my life. May You give me and all Your creatures a heart of compassion. May all cruelty, all cruel regimes, vanish from the earth like smoke. Wash clean our heart that we may serve You with truth, and may the inclinations of all hearts be united to love and revere Your Name.

EIRUV TAVSHILIN

DIRECTIONS: When the first Seder falls on a Wednesday night, *Eiruv Tavshilin* is observed by all who do not cook on Shabbat, so that preparation of food for Shabbat may take place during the holiday. Set aside a cooked dish and some matzah to be eaten on Shabbat. This permits additional food for Shabbat to be prepared during Pesach. When the food is set aside, the following is said:

בָּרוּךְ אַתָּה יְיָ אֱלֹהֵינוּ מֶלֶךְ הָעוֹלָם אֲשֶׁר קִדְּשָׁנוּ
בְּמִצְוֹתָיו וְצִוָּנוּ עַל מִצְוַת עֵרוּב:

Ba-ruch a-ta A-do-nai E-lo-hei-nu me-lech ha-o-lam a-sher ki-de-sha-nu be-mitz-vo-tav ve-tzi-va-nu al mitz-vat ei-ruv.

You are praised, Adonai our God, Monarch of time and space, Who shares Your holiness with us through Your mitzvot, and now bestows on us the mitzvah of *Eiruv*.

בַּהֲדִין עֵרוּבָה יְהֵא שְׁרֵא לָנָא לְמֵפָא וּלְבַשָּׁלָא וּלְאַטְמָנָא
וּלְאַדְלָקָא שְׁרָגָא וּלְמֶעְבַּד כָּל צָרְכָנָה מִיּוֹמָא טָבָא
לְשַׁבְּתָא לָנוּ וּלְכָל יִשְׂרָאֵל הַדָּרִים בָּעִיר הַזֹּאת:

By means of this Eiruv, we and all who dwell in this community become permitted to bake, to cook, to warm food, to kindle and adjust lights, and to make all the preparations for Shabbat during Yomtov.

CONTENTS OF THE TALE

LIGHTING OF CANDLES

Reflections

We are about to light the candles,
But it is not we who light them.
We shall strike the match
But God will bring forth light.
May God bring forth light from us
As we tell how God brought forth our people
From the darkness of Egypt's burning days
Into the radiance of this joyous night.

DIRECTIONS: The candles are lit and the following be-ra-chah (blessing) is offered:

בָּרוּךְ אַתָּה יְיָ אֱלֹהֵינוּ מֶלֶךְ הָעוֹלָם. אֲשֶׁר קִדְּשָׁנוּ
בְּמִצְוֹתָיו וְצִוָּנוּ לְהַדְלִיק נֵר שֶׁל [שַׁבָּת וְשֶׁל] יוֹם טוֹב:

Ba-ruch a-ta A-do-nai E-lo-hei-nu me-lech ha-o-lam
a-sher kid-e-sha-nu be-mitz-vo-tav, ve-tzi-va-nu le-
had-lik ner shel [Sha-bat ve-shel] yom tov.

Praised are You, Adonai our God, Monarch of time and
space, who has brought us into Your holy presence through
Your mitzvot, commanding us to bring into this room the
good light You formed for [Shabbat and] festive days.

*(Those who recite the She-he-che-ya-nu prayer now need not repeat it
during Kiddush. She-he-che-ya-nu is offered only on the first two
nights.)*

בָּרוּךְ אַתָּה יְיָ אֱלֹהֵינוּ מֶלֶךְ הָעוֹלָם שֶׁהֶחֱיָנוּ וְקִיְּמָנוּ
וְהִגִּיעָנוּ לַזְּמַן הַזֶּה:

Ba-ruch a-ta A-do-nai E-lo-hei-nu me-lech ha-o-lam
she-he-che-ya-nu ve-ki-ye-ma-nu ve-hi-gi-ya-nu la-ze-
man ha-zeh.

Praised are You, Adonai our God, Monarch of time and
space, who has kept us alive, upheld us, and brought us to
this holy time once more.

קַדֵשׁ

KADESH

Say Kiddush o'er the grape
And taste how sweet was our escape

Introduction by the Song

יַשְׁקֵנִי מִנְּשִׁיקוֹת פִּיהוּ כִּי־טוֹבִים דֹּדֶיךָ מִיָּיִן:

דּוֹדִי לִי וַאֲנִי לוֹ הָרֹעֶה בַּשּׁוֹשַׁנִּים:

O kiss me with the kisses of your mouth,
For your love is better than wine!
My beloved, you are mine and I am yours,
O shepherd of our lilyfields.

(Song of Songs 1:2, 2:16)

Reflections (Choose one or more)

Why do we drink four cups on this night?

1) It is the first reminder that only the Jews, who suffered so much under the Romans, have preserved the customs of the Roman meal: reclining when we drink, two cups before the meal and two after, dipping one kind of food into another before eating. But since the ancient Romans exist no longer, banished to oblivion for their cruelty and their ostentation, why do we continue their custom? Perhaps as a reminder that however human beings may misuse the products of God's Creation, it is up to us to help redeem them, to restore the holiness for which God created them. Thus we have transformed the ostentatious meal of an arrogant oppressor into the modest matzah feast of the (rescued) oppressed. Part of the transformation takes place through the taste of the wine itself, changing an ordinary night into the holy time of Passover.

2) Four is an important number in the Seder: four cups, four children, four questions, four matriarchs in the Who Knows One. It is an important number in Jewish thought as well: four corners (*arba kanfot*) of the tallit, four corners of the world, four kinds of fruit from goodly trees for Sukkot. Many numbers play a special role in religious literature. Part of

the special quality of four may derive from the four points of the compass, or the four sides of the square, thus suggesting completeness and sufficiency.

3) In the sixth chapter of Exodus (verses 6 and 7), God makes four promises to Israel which flow out of God's covenant with us: *Ve-ho-tzei-ti* (I will bring you out from under the burdens of Mitzrayim), *Ve-hi-tzal-ti* (I will deliver you from their service), *Ve-ga-al-ti* (I will redeem you with an outstretched arm and great judgments), *Ve-la-kach-ti* (I will take you to Me for a people and I will become God for you). Traditionally, each cup represents one of these promises.

But in verse 8 of Chapter 6 there is a fifth promise: *Ve-he-vei-ti* (I shall bring you to the Land), which, by Seder night, had not been fulfilled. The debate over whether this fifth promise should be celebrated by a cup of its own led to the decision to leave the answer to Elijah, herald of the messianic coming. Hence the custom of the Cup for Elijah and the messianic "fifth cup."

A Further Reflection

A great teacher, Rav Moshe Poleyoff, once explained the difference between drinking for the sake of the mitzvah and drinking that leads to drunkenness. If one is empty inside and expects the wine to supply the happiness, the wine only leads to hopeless abandon and inebriation. But if one is filled with joy and wishes to express that joy through drink, then the wine represents a *simchah shel mitzvah* (the joy of the mitzvah)—and the consumption of the wine itself becomes a mitzvah. That is the kind of drinking that takes place at the Passover Seder.

*   *   *   *   *

THE FIRST CUP: Relief from Our Burdens

DIRECTIONS: Pour wine into each person's vessel for the First Cup, *Ve-ho-tzei-ti*, "I will bring you out from under the burdens of Mitzrayim" (Exodus 6:6). The leader, or whoever is making Kiddush, offers the following words, adding the bracketed passages on Friday night, Shabbat:

[וַיְהִי־עֶרֶב וַיְהִי־בֹקֶר]

יוֹם הַשִּׁשִּׁי. וַיְכֻלּוּ הַשָּׁמַיִם וְהָאָרֶץ וְכָל־צְבָאָם: וַיְכַל
אֱלֹהִים בַּיּוֹם הַשְּׁבִיעִי מְלַאכְתּוֹ אֲשֶׁר עָשָׂה. וַיִּשְׁבֹּת
בַּיּוֹם הַשְּׁבִיעִי מִכָּל־מְלַאכְתּוֹ אֲשֶׁר עָשָׂה: וַיְבָרֶךְ אֱלֹהִים

אֶת־יוֹם הַשְּׁבִיעִי וַיְקַדֵּשׁ אֹתוֹ כִּי בוֹ שָׁבַת מִכָּל־מְלַאכְתּוֹ
אֲשֶׁר בָּרָא אֱלֹהִים לַעֲשׂוֹת:

[Va-ye-hi e-rev va-ye-hi vo-ker yom va-shi-shi. Va-ye-chu-lu ha-sha-ma-yim ve-ha-a-retz ve-chol tze-va-am. Va-ye-chal E-lo-him ba-yom ha-she-vi-i me-lach-to a-sher a-sa, va-yish-bot ba-yom ha-she-vi-i mi-kol me-lach-to a-sher a-sa. Va-ye-va-rech E-lo-him et yom ha-she-vi-i va-ye-ka-desh o-to, ki vo sha-vat mi-kol me-lach-to a-sher ba-ra E-lo-him la-a-sot.]

[And there was evening and there was morning, the sixth day. And when the heavens and all their host were finished, God completed on the seventh day the work which God had made. And God imbued the seventh day with blessing and holiness, for on it God rested from all the divine work which God created.]

סַבְרֵי חֲבֵרַי וַחֲבֵרוֹתַי:

Sav-rei cha-vei-rai ve-cha-vei-ro-tai:

With your permission, my friends:

(It is a Sephardic custom for all guests here to say, "L'cha-yim!" meaning, "To long life!")

בָּרוּךְ אַתָּה יְיָ אֱלֹהֵינוּ מֶלֶךְ הָעוֹלָם. בּוֹרֵא פְּרִי הַגָּפֶן:
(On the first two nights say:)

בָּרוּךְ אַתָּה יְיָ אֱלֹהֵינוּ מֶלֶךְ הָעוֹלָם. אֲשֶׁר בָּחַר בָּנוּ
מִכָּל־עָם. וְרוֹמְמָנוּ מִכָּל־לָשׁוֹן. וְקִדְּשָׁנוּ בְּמִצְוֹתָיו.
וַתִּתֶּן־לָנוּ יְיָ אֱלֹהֵינוּ בְּאַהֲבָה [שַׁבָּתוֹת לִמְנוּחָה וּ]
מוֹעֲדִים לְשִׂמְחָה חַגִּים וּזְמַנִּים לְשָׂשׂוֹן. אֶת־יוֹם [הַשַּׁבָּת
הַזֶּה וְאֶת־יוֹם] חַג הַמַּצּוֹת הַזֶּה זְמַן חֵרוּתֵנוּ [בְּאַהֲבָה]
מִקְרָא־קֹדֶשׁ זֵכֶר לִיצִיאַת מִצְרָיִם. כִּי בָנוּ בָחַרְתָּ וְאוֹתָנוּ
קִדַּשְׁתָּ מִכָּל־הָעַמִּים [וְשַׁבָּת] וּמוֹעֲדֵי קָדְשֶׁךָ [בְּאַהֲבָה
וּבְרָצוֹן] בְּשִׂמְחָה וּבְשָׂשׂוֹן הִנְחַלְתָּנוּ. בָּרוּךְ אַתָּה יְיָ
מְקַדֵּשׁ [הַשַּׁבָּת וְ]יִשְׂרָאֵל וְהַזְּמַנִּים:

Ba-ruch a-ta A-do-nai E-lo-hei-nu me-lech ha-o-lam, bo-rei pe-ri ha-ga-fen.

Ba-ruch a-ta A-do-nai E-lo-hei-nu me-lech ha-o-lam a-sher ba-char ba-nu mi-kol am, ve-ro-me-ma-nu mi-kol la-shon ve-kid-e-sha-nu be-mitz-vo-tav. Va-ti-ten la-nu A-do-nai E-lo-hei-nu be-a-ha-va [Sha-ba-tot li-me-nu-cha u-] mo-a-dim le-sim-cha, cha-gim u-ze-ma-nim le-sa-son, et yom [ha-Sha-bat ha-zeh ve-et yom] Chag Ha-Ma-tzot ha-zeh, ze-man chei-ru-tei-nu [be-a-ha-vah] mik-ra ko-desh, ze-cher li-tzi-at Mitz-ra-yim. Ki va-nu va-char-ta ve-o-ta-nu ki-dash-ta mi-kol ha-a-mim [ve-Sha-bat] u-mo-a-dei kod-she-cha [be-a-ha-vah u-ve-ra-tzon] be-sim-cha u-ve-sa-son hin-chal-ta-nu. Ba-ruch a-ta A-do-nai me-ka-desh [ha-Sha-bat ve-] Yis-ra-el ve-ha-ze-ma-nim.

Praised are You, Adonai our God, Monarch of time and space, creator of this fruit of the vine.

Praised are You, Adonai our God, Monarch of time and space, who chose us for a relationship different from other peoples, lifting us who know the tongue of Creation above the speakers of ordinary language, enabling us to encounter holiness through Your mitzvot, giving us lovingly [Shabbat for rest,] holidays for joy, festivals and special times for celebration, particularly this [Shabbat and this] Matzah Festival, this time of freedom [given in love], this holy gathering, this re-enactment of our going out from Mitzrayim. For it is You who have chosen us, You who have shared Your holiness with us, in a different way than with other peoples. For with [Shabbat and] festive revelations of Your holiness have You dowered us, happily and joyfully [, lovingly and willingly]. You are praised, Adonai, who imbues with holiness [Shabbat,] Israel, and the special times.

(On Saturday night, mo-tza-ei Sha-bat, add the following prayers marking the division, Havdalah, between Shabbat and the festival:)

(בָּרוּךְ אַתָּה יְיָ אֱלֹהֵינוּ מֶלֶךְ הָעוֹלָם. בּוֹרֵא מְאוֹרֵי הָאֵשׁ:

בָּרוּךְ אַתָּה יְיָ אֱלֹהֵינוּ מֶלֶךְ הָעוֹלָם. הַמַּבְדִּיל בֵּין קֹדֶשׁ לְחוֹל. בֵּין אוֹר לְחשֶׁךְ. בֵּין יִשְׂרָאֵל לָעַמִּים. בֵּין יוֹם

הַשְּׁבִיעִי לְשֵׁשֶׁת יְמֵי הַמַּעֲשֶׂה: בֵּין קְדֻשַּׁת שַׁבָּת לִקְדֻשַּׁת
יוֹם טוֹב הִבְדַּלְתָּ וְאֶת־יוֹם הַשְּׁבִיעִי מִשֵּׁשֶׁת יְמֵי־
הַמַּעֲשֶׂה קִדַּשְׁתָּ. הִבְדַּלְתָּ וְקִדַּשְׁתָּ אֶת־עַמְּךָ יִשְׂרָאֵל
בִּקְדֻשָּׁתֶךָ. בָּרוּךְ אַתָּה יְיָ הַמַּבְדִּיל בֵּין קֹדֶשׁ לְקֹדֶשׁ:)

(Ba-ruch a-ta A-do-nai E-lo-hei-nu me-lech ha-o-lam,
bo-rei me-o-rei ha-esh.

(Ba-ruch a-ta A-do-nai E-lo-hei-nu me-lech ha-o-lam,
ha-mav-dil bein ko-desh le-chol, bein or le-cho-shech,
bein Yis-ra-el la-a-mim, bein yom ha-she-vi-i le-she-shet
ye-mei ha-ma-a-seh. Bein ke-du-shat Sha-bat li-ke-du-
shat yom tov hiv-dal-ta, ve-et yom ha-she-vi-i mi-she-
shet ye-mei ha-ma-a-seh ki-dash-ta, hiv-dal-ta ve-ki-
dash-ta et am-cha Yis-ra-el bi-ke-du-sha-te-cha. Ba-ruch
a-ta A-do-nai, ha-mav-dil bein ko-desh le-ko-desh.)

(You are praised, Adonai our God, Monarch of time and
space, who creates the lights of fire.

You are praised, Adonai our God, Monarch of time and
space, who distinguishes between holy and ordinary, light
and darkness, Israel and the peoples, the seventh day and the
six days of activity, the holiness of Shabbat and the holiness
of a festival. You have imbued the seventh day with greater
holiness than the six days of activity, You have poured some
of Your holiness into Your people Israel. You are praised,
Adonai, who distinguishes among the vintages of holiness.)

*(If you did not offer the She-he-che-ya-nu prayer while lighting
candles, do so now before drinking the wine. She-he-che-ya-nu is said
only on the first two nights.)*

בָּרוּךְ אַתָּה יְיָ אֱלֹהֵינוּ מֶלֶךְ הָעוֹלָם. שֶׁהֶחֱיָנוּ. וְקִיְּמָנוּ.
וְהִגִּיעָנוּ לַזְּמַן הַזֶּה:

Ba-ruch a-ta A-do-nai E-lo-hei-nu me-lech ha-o-lam,
she-he-che-ya-nu ve-ki-ye-ma-nu ve-hi-gi-a-nu la-ze-
man ha-zeh.

Praised are You, Adonai our God, Monarch of time and

space, who has kept us alive, upheld us, and brought us to this holy time once more.

DIRECTIONS: Drink from the First Cup. *Ve-ho-tzei-ti*, "I will bring you out," while reclining to the left, tasting the holy joy of this festival night.

U-RE-CHATZ

Dip Hands

Reflections

On frozen ponds, the warm kiss of spring turns ice to flowing water, as the loving power of God turned the ice of Pharaoh's heart into the flowing exodus of Israel through the waters of redemption.

How many waters flow through the Pesach tales—Moses in the bullrushes, the Nile turned to blood, the splitting of the Sea, Marah's bitter waters sweetened, the well the rabbis believed followed the Israelites in the wilderness in Miriam's honor.

Their waters are ours. Their rivers run into our cups. Let us all splash for a moment in the common stream of life.

(U-she-av-tem ma-yim, *page 143, may be sung here.*)

DIRECTIONS: Using a cup or a pitcher, the leader should pour fresh water over each hand, either on behalf of the Seder participants, or in company with them. Participants may also be encouraged to pour the water over the hands of their neighbors, presenting them with a symbolic gift of life. The washing is done in silence, without a blessing.

KARPAS

Then Greens We Dip

Reflections

As You brought Israel forth from the dark and narrow places of Mitzrayim, so every spring You bring forth green shoots of life from the dark earth. To hold aloft a sprig of new life is to hold aloft a people blessed with new life—Israelites sprouted from Mitzrayim, refuseniks from the Soviet Union, Beta Yisrael from Ethiopia.

Yet, for each sprig that breaks through the soil to turn green beneath the sun, there are so many that remain hidden in the darkness, in hostile lands, in the narrow places of homelessness and hunger. We rejoice that there are so many places where the world is green; we mourn all those places where it is not.

And so we wash the green in the salt water of all the tears that flow in those places, and in the salt water of the sea You split as a reminder that one day, tears shall only flow in joy.

קוֹל דּוֹדִי הִנֵּה־זֶה בָּא. מְדַלֵּג עַל־הֶהָרִים מְקַפֵּץ עַל־הַגְּבָעוֹת: דּוֹמֶה דוֹדִי לִצְבִי אוֹ לְעֹפֶר הָאַיָּלִים. הִנֵּה־זֶה עוֹמֵד אַחַר כָּתְלֵנוּ מַשְׁגִּיחַ מִן־הַחַלֹּנוֹת מֵצִיץ מִן־הַחֲרַכִּים: עָנָה דוֹדִי וְאָמַר לִי. קוּמִי לָךְ רַעְיָתִי יָפָתִי וּלְכִי־לָךְ: כִּי־הִנֵּה הַסְּתָו עָבָר. הַגֶּשֶׁם חָלַף הָלַךְ לוֹ: הַנִּצָּנִים נִרְאוּ בָאָרֶץ עֵת הַזָּמִיר הִגִּיעַ. וְקוֹל הַתּוֹר נִשְׁמַע בְּאַרְצֵנוּ: הַתְּאֵנָה חָנְטָה פַגֶּיהָ וְהַגְּפָנִים סְמָדַר נָתְנוּ רֵיחַ. קוּמִי לְכִי רַעְיָתִי יָפָתִי וּלְכִי־לָךְ:

My beloved's voice! Look, it's come
Skipping over the mountains, leaping over the hills!
My beloved is like a gazelle, a young deer,
Look—standing behind our wall, watching at the window,
Peering through the lattice.

My beloved responds to me: Arise, my companion,
My splendid one, come away!

For look, winter has passed,
The rain, it has transformed the earth and gone away,
Now buds appear on the earth, the time of singing has come,
The voice of the turtledove is heard in our land!

The fig tree presents her figs,
The blossoming vines uncork their fragrance,
Arise, my companion, my splendid one,
Come away!

(Song of Songs 2:8–13)

* * * * *

(Melodies from the Song of Songs, page 143, may be sung here.)

An Alternative Karpas

In the year 5745, the year of Operation Moses, thousands of Ethiopian Jews came home to Israel. To help them adjust to their arrival in a land far from Ethiopia's famine, they were fed simple foods so that their frail bodies, racked with hunger, would not be subjected to the shock that so many victims of the concentration camps suffered when they were fed regular food too soon after their liberation.

As a result of this concern, the first meal of the Ethiopian Jews was boiled potatoes, the fruit of the earth, a new vegetable of redemption. Even this potato, though, is more than many people have to eat. Let it be a symbol of our resolve to share our bounty with the hungry in our own community and around the world, before too many more people are reduced to such a condition that all their bodies can tolerate is a potato.

DIRECTIONS: Dip a vegetable, grown in the earth, into salt water and say:

בָּרוּךְ אַתָּה יְיָ אֱלֹהֵינוּ מֶלֶךְ הָעוֹלָם. בּוֹרֵא פְּרִי הָאֲדָמָה:

Ba-ruch a-ta A-do-nai E-lo-hei-nu me-lech ha-o-lam bo-rei pe-ri ha-a-da-mah.

You are praised, Adonai our God, Monarch of time and space, who creates this fruit of the earth.

YA-CHATZ

And in two the matzah rip;
Take the cover, put half inside
And the other half now hide

Reader

Bring forth the matzah from its hiding place!

DIRECTIONS: Leader removes the middle matzah from its cover.

Company

Bring forth Israel from slavery!

Reader

Break one in two, leave two within the covering!

DIRECTIONS: Leader breaks middle matzah in two uneven pieces.

Company

Celebrate the double portion of manna for Shabbat and festivals, the double portion of bread upon the Temple altar: two whole loaves, however divided the Jewish people may be!

Reader

Hide one piece of matzah, leave the other longing for its mate!

DIRECTIONS: Leader hides the larger piece of the broken matzah as the afikomon, replacing the smaller piece between the two remaining matzot.

Reflections

The Matzah Longing for Its Mate

עַל־מִשְׁכָּבִי בַּלֵּילוֹת בִּקַּשְׁתִּי אֵת שֶׁאָהֲבָה נַפְשִׁי.
בִּקַּשְׁתִּיו וְלֹא מְצָאתִיו: אָקוּמָה נָּא וַאֲסוֹבְבָה בָעִיר
בַּשְּׁוָקִים וּבָרְחֹבוֹת אֲבַקְשָׁה אֵת שֶׁאָהֲבָה נַפְשִׁי. בִּקַּשְׁתִּיו
וְלֹא מְצָאתִיו:

In the night
From the place where I reclined
I have sought the one I love.
I sought, but found I not!
I shall arise now and go around the city,
In the streets and in the squares,
To seek the one I love.

I sought, but found I not!

(Song of Songs 3:1-2)

*   *   *   *   *

The Broken Matzah

No word is spoken, no benediction is uttered before *Yachatz*, the breaking of the middle matzah. It is a silent, reflective act wherein part of the matzah is concealed to be searched out towards the end of the Pesach meal, before the blessings that conclude the meal may be recited.

It is the larger part of the middle matzah that is concealed. For more is hidden than is revealed. Within us, individually and collectively, there are prayers to be fulfilled, promises to be redeemed. We are, like the broken matzah, incomplete.

We prepared for Pesach in the night, searching for the hidden leavened bread; we will end the seder in the night, searching for the unleavened bread. To know there is concealment is to know that there is always something to be completed, to be searched out, to be found.

*   *   *   *   *

Wrapping matzah in the cover reminds us of our mothers and fathers on their way out of Mitzrayim, who wrapped up the dough before it had a chance to leaven and carried it with their kneading-troughs on their shoulders (Exodus 12:34).

It also reminds us that if you are poor, if you do not know where your next meal is coming from, you do not eat everything that is in front of you. You hide a bit of food, a piece of bread, to make sure you won't starve after this meal is over. *Yachatz* reminds us that this is Chag Ha-Matzot, the Festival of Poor People's Bread.

*   *   *   *   *

In the Talmud (Berachot 39b) Rav Papa says that the matzah fulfills the command to eat *lechem oni*, poor people's crumbs (Deuteronomy 16:3), while Rav Abba says it fulfills the command for *lechem mishneh*, the extra loaf commemorating the double portion of manna for Shabbat and festivals. The three matzot are a compromise which fulfills both interpretations, ensuring that despite the broken piece, we always have two whole matzot.

Yet, even as we ourselves are graced with an extra loaf, on Pesach it is a loaf of poor people's bread—a double portion of poverty: not only our people's in Egypt, but also our own family's on the immigrant ships, or our unsheltered neighbors' on the streets of our own cities. How can there be such poverty in the world in the midst of so much surplus? What can we ourselves do to right the balance?

מַגִּיד
MA-GID

Tell the tale of slavery's woe
And how God let our people go

Reflections

Lover's Journey: A Midrash on the Song of Songs

(The lines in roman type are from Song of Songs 2:8-13; the lines in italic type are from Song of Songs Rabba, a midrashic commentary.)

Hark, behold! My beloved is coming!
    Moses is telling us we shall be delivered!
    But God told Abraham we would be slaves four hundred
      years,
    And only two hundred ten have passed!
My beloved is coming,
Leaping over the mountains,
    Leaping over the centuries,
    Shortening the years till our redemption!
Skipping over the hills,
    Ignoring the gods we worship on the pagan hills;
My beloved is like a gazelle, a young deer,
    Leaping from Egypt to the Reed Sea,
    From the Reed Sea to Sinai,
    From Sinai to the future redemption of the world!
Look—standing behind our wall,
    Present still behind the Western Wall of the Temple,
    Beckoning to the redemption yet to come,
Looking in through the windows
    Letting in the light of Torah from Mount Sinai,
Peering through the lattice
    Looking at us not only as we are,
    But seeing in us all the qualities we have inherited
    From the matriarchs and patriarchs whose deeds are in our
      blood.
My beloved spoke and said to me,
    Speaking through Moses, saying to Miriam and the genera-
      tion in Egypt,

*Speaking through Daniel, saying to Ezra and the generation
    returned from Exile,*
*Speaking through Elijah, saying to the Messiah and to us
    who are still to be redeemed:*
Rise up my love, my splendid one, and come away.

For behold the winter is past,
    Just as the two hundred ten years have passed,
The rain is over and gone,
    Just as the Babylonian captivity has gone,
    So the oppressions of our time too will pass away.
The flowers have appeared on the earth,
    Those who will conquer our oppressors have already appeared,
And the time of singing has come,
    The time of the song of Israel's redemption has come,
    The rule of heaven is to be revealed,
The voice of the turtledove is heard in our land,
    The voice of the tourguide into our land is heard,
    *Calling us from the wilderness, from Babylonia, from exile
        anywhere we are enslaved,*
    To go forth into the land God has promised us all.
The fig tree has put forth ripe figs,
    The nations will put forth their wicked for punishment
    *And we shall again put forth our first-fruits on the altar of
        Your house,*
And the vines in blossom put forth their fragrance,
    Those who repent (how sweet they are!) shall be delivered,
    *And we shall again put forth offerings of fragrant wine on
        the altar of Your house.*
Arise my love, my splendid one, and come away.

*   *   *   *   *

Four majestic acts have marked our Seder so far: sipping the
holiness of the day, pouring living water over our flesh, dipping
spring greens into salt water, splitting and hiding the bread of
poverty and freedom. Yet these are but the prologue to the core of
the Seder, which we now begin: telling the tale. We shall uncover
the matzah and welcome the poor, ask the Four Questions, bring
in the Four Children, and recount the epic of redemption. The
true secret of Pesach, like the secret inside each one of us, emerges
in the telling of our stories. The broken matzah starts our tale.

HA LACHMA ANYA

DIRECTIONS: Turn down the covering of the matzot, showing the broken matzah to everyone, then raise up the Seder Plate with the symbolic foods.

הָא לַחְמָא עַנְיָא דִי־אֲכָלוּ אֲבָהָתַנָא (וְאִמְּהָתַנָא) בְּאַרְעָא
דְמִצְרָיִם. כָּל־דִּכְפִין יֵיתֵי וְיֵכוֹל. כָּל־דִּצְרִיךְ יֵיתֵי וְיִפְסַח.
הָשַׁתָּא הָכָא. לְשָׁנָה הַבָּאָה בְּאַרְעָא דְיִשְׂרָאֵל. הָשַׁתָּא
עַבְדֵי. לְשָׁנָה הַבָּאָה בְּנֵי (וּבְנוֹת) חוֹרִין:

Ha lach-ma an-ya di a-cha-lu a-va-ha-ta-na (ve-i-ma-ha-ta-na) be-ar-ah de-Mitz-ra-yim. Kol dich-fin yei-tei ve-yei-chol, kol ditz-rich yei-tei ve-yif-sach. Ha-sha-ta ha-cha, la-sha-na ha-ba-ah be-ar-a de-Yis-ra-el. Ha-sha-ta av-dei, la-sha-na ha-ba-ah be-nei (u-ve-not) cho-rin.

Reflections

As this invitation was originally offered in Aramaic, the people's tongue, so that all might feel welcome at the Seder, so we extend it now in the people's tongue of the land in which we live, that everyone here tonight may know that we want you at our table:

*   *   *   *   *

This is the bread of poverty, the bread of affliction,
Our fathers and mothers ate it in the land of Mitzrayim,
Which means the land of Constriction, of Narrowness.
Would that anyone in need might come and share our
       Pesach!
This year we are here,
In the coming year may we be in the Land of Israel.
This year we are slaves
In the coming year may we all be free!

Reflections

Mitzrayim is not just a place on an ancient map
Where a narrow strait blocks the way between two seas,
Mitzrayim is a place in us
Where a narrow strait blocks the sea which is our soul
From reaching the Sea which is its source.

We have built that strait
From all that has enslaved us
All the crudities we worship
All the greed that blocks the arteries of our life.

And so,
When our soul laps longingly at the edge,
The sludge of our grasping days
Pushes it, gasping, back,
Choking it off, day by day, from the sea
Which is its life.

To eat this bread of affliction
Is to take a bite out of that which afflicts us,
To tear into the sludge of our enslavement
And gnaw away at it, layer by layer,
Until we clear through the straits
A channel for our soul
To flow back again into its source.

At this moment our soul is still enslaved,
Before this night ends, may it once again breathe free!

* * * * *

(The Jewish inmates of the Bergen-Belsen concentration camp had no matzah to eat for Pesach in 1944. On the counsel of their rabbis they offered this prayer:)

Our God in Heaven, behold it is evident and known to You that it is our desire to do Your will and to celebrate the Festival of Passover by eating Matzah and by observing the prohibition of chametz. But our heart is pained that the enslavement prevents us, and we are in danger of our lives. Behold we are prepared and ready to fulfill Your commandment: "And you shall live by them and not die by them . . ." (rabbinic comment to Leviticus 18:5). Therefore our prayer to You is that You may keep us alive and save us and rescue us speedily so that we may observe Your commandments and do Your will and serve You with a perfect heart. Amen.

* * * * *

OPTIONAL DIRECTIONS: A person sitting near an empty chair holds up a piece of matzah and reads the following:

This is the bread for the person who is not here:
The Jew in the Soviet Union, learning Torah behind closed curtains,
Savoring hidden freedom like matzah covered by the cloth,

Waiting, like the afikomon, to be redeemed;
The Jew in hostile Arab lands, in impoverished Ethiopia,
Who on this very night
Praise the God who promised them their freedom,
And thus they know, deep inside their souls,
That it will come.

O God whom we call Mikveh Yisrael, Hope of Israel,
Let us know the hope that has sustained our sisters and brothers
    through the years,
Let us look not only at the empty chair
But at the plate full of matzot,
The plate full of hope that freedom is not a fairytale,
But a tale as real as it is old.
As we tell the tale tonight, let us fill the chair with our hope
That next year a living person from Mitzrayim will be sitting here,
Here in this room,
Here in Eretz Yisrael,
Here in freedom.

THE FOUR PUZZLEMENTS (The Four Questions)

DIRECTIONS: Pour wine or grape juice for each person's second cup, the Cup of Deliverance. Cover the three matzot while attention is being paid to the wine.

Reflections

Once each of us was the youngest
Trained to ask the Four Questions, the Fier Kashes, the Ma Nishtanah
On this night of praise for God's wonderful acts.

We practiced for weeks, were nervous for days,
When the time came, all eyes turned toward us—
And however we did, however we stumbled,
Everyone beamed, pinched our cheeks, shook their heads
At How Wonderful we were

(Except for those younger than we,
Impatient for their turn,
Or those a bit older,
Resentful that no one was beaming at them).

Now we too have grown older,
Our places too have been taken,
The beams have passed to other eyes.

It's good to grow up, to leave some struggles behind.

Still,

It wouldn't hurt someone to remember,
To recall our nervous voices once again,
To share our smile of triumph at the last *ha-lai-la ha-zeh* . . . .
Why is this night different from those other nights?

It feels good to be wonderful.

* * * * *

DIRECTIONS: It is customary for the youngest child present to ask the Four Questions. Anyone may ask them, however, including a single person celebrating a Seder alone.

מַה־נִּשְׁתַּנָּה הַלַּיְלָה הַזֶּה מִכָּל־הַלֵּילוֹת.

1. שֶׁבְּכָל־הַלֵּילוֹת אָנוּ אוֹכְלִין חָמֵץ וּמַצָּה. הַלַּיְלָה הַזֶּה
כֻּלּוֹ מַצָּה:

2. שֶׁבְּכָל־הַלֵּילוֹת אָנוּ אוֹכְלִין שְׁאָר יְרָקוֹת. הַלַּיְלָה הַזֶּה
מָרוֹר:

3. שֶׁבְּכָל־הַלֵּילוֹת אֵין אָנוּ מַטְבִּילִין אֲפִילוּ פַּעַם אֶחָת.
הַלַּיְלָה הַזֶּה שְׁתֵּי פְעָמִים:

4. שֶׁבְּכָל־הַלֵּילוֹת אָנוּ אוֹכְלִין בֵּין יוֹשְׁבִין וּבֵין מְסֻבִּין.
הַלַּיְלָה הַזֶּה כֻּלָּנוּ מְסֻבִּין:

Mah nish-ta-nah ha-lai-lah ha-zeh mi-kol ha-lei-lot:

1. Sheh-be-chol ha-lei-lot a-nu och-lin cha-metz u-ma-tzah,
ha-lai-lah ha-zeh ku-lo ma-tzah?

2. Sheh-be-chol ha-lei-lot a-nu och-lin she-ar ye-ra-kot; ha-
lai-lah ha-zeh ma-ror?

3. Sheh-be-chol ha-lei-lot ein a-nu mat-bi-lin a-fi-lu pa-am
eh-chat; ha-lai-lah ha-zeh she-tei fe-a-mim?

4. Sheh-be-chol ha-lei-lot a-nu och-lin bein yosh-vin u-vein
me-su-bin; ha-lai-lah ha-zeh ku-la-nu me-su-bin?

Why is this night different from all other nights:

1. In that, on all other nights, we eat leavened bread (chametz) and matzah; on this night, only matzah?

2. In that, on all other nights, we eat other vegetables; on this night, a bitter vegetable (maror)?

3. In that, on all other nights, we do not dip even once; on this night, twice (greens in salt water, maror in charoset)?

4. In that, on all other nights, we eat either sitting upright or reclining; on this night, all of us recline?

Reflections: On Answering the Questions

Some people say children's questions should always be answered immediately and fully. But every child knows that doesn't always happen. "Can we have a picnic tomorrow?" "We'll see." "Where do babies come from?" "Inside their mommies."

Children often give similar answers. "What happened in school today?" "Nothing." "What were you and your friend doing in your room?" "Playing." And surely God doesn't always respond to questions right away—or at least, in the way we expect.

The Haggadah, too, responds to the Four Puzzlements in a puzzling way. It doesn't talk about chametz and matzah, or about maror; those responses come later, just before the meal, in Rabban Gamliel's story. And it doesn't explain dipping or reclining at all—except, as with all four questions, by telling the story of the Exodus.

Thus, in response to material questions—"Why do we eat matzah and maror and dip twice and recline?"—we are given historical answers, spiritual answers; answers, the Talmud tells us (Pesachim 116a), that begin with degradation and culminate in praise.

What was our degradation? The Talmudic sage Shmuel said, "*Avadim ha-yinu*, we were slaves." And what is our praise? That we "enlarge on the tale of the going-out of Mitzrayim." Shmuel's opponent in Talmudic argument, Rav, has another set of answers that we will read later on.

*   *   *   *   *

AVADIM HA-YINU

DIRECTIONS: Uncover the matzot during the recital of the story which tells us why we eat them.

עֲבָדִים הָיִינוּ לְפַרְעֹה בְּמִצְרָיִם. וַיּוֹצִיאֵנוּ יְיָ אֱלֹהֵינוּ
מִשָּׁם בְּיָד חֲזָקָה וּבִזְרוֹעַ נְטוּיָה: וְאִלּוּ לֹא הוֹצִיא הַקָּדוֹשׁ
בָּרוּךְ הוּא אֶת־אֲבוֹתֵינוּ (וְאֶת־אִמּוֹתֵינוּ) מִמִּצְרָיִם. הֲרֵי
אָנוּ וּבָנֵינוּ וּבְנֵי בָנֵינוּ מְשֻׁעְבָּדִים הָיִינוּ לְפַרְעֹה בְּמִצְרָיִם.
וַאֲפִילוּ כֻּלָּנוּ חֲכָמִים. כֻּלָּנוּ נְבוֹנִים. כֻּלָּנוּ זְקֵנִים. כֻּלָּנוּ
יוֹדְעִים אֶת־הַתּוֹרָה. מִצְוָה עָלֵינוּ לְסַפֵּר בִּיצִיאַת
מִצְרָיִם. וְכָל־הַמַּרְבֶּה לְסַפֵּר בִּיצִיאַת מִצְרַיִם הֲרֵי־זֶה
מְשֻׁבָּח:

We were slaves to Pharaoh in Mitzrayim, and then Adonai our God brought us out of there with a mighty hand and an outstretched arm. But if the Blessed Holy One had not brought our ancestors out of Mitzrayim, we and our children and our children's children would still be enslaved to Pharaoh in Mitzrayim.

So, even if all of us were wise, all of us understanding, all of us old and venerable, all of us learned in Torah, it would still be a mitzvah for us to tell the story of the Going-out of Mitzrayim. And everyone who enlarges on the Tale of the Going-out of Mitzrayim deserves praise.

Song: A-va-dim ha-yi-nu, ha-yinu, a-ta ve-nei cho-rin, ve-nei cho-rin.
(We were slaves; now we are free.)

THE RABBIS OF BENEI BERAK

(Among the people who struggled with the meaning of our slavery are these five sages, who have for centuries been singled out for praise for elaborating so long on the story of the Exodus:)

מַעֲשֶׂה בְּרַבִּי אֱלִיעֶזֶר וְרַבִּי יְהוֹשֻׁעַ וְרַבִּי אֶלְעָזָר בֶּן־

עֲזַרְיָה וְרַבִּי עֲקִיבָא וְרַבִּי טַרְפוֹן שֶׁהָיוּ מְסֻבִּין בִּבְנֵי בְרַק.
וְהָיוּ מְסַפְּרִים בִּיצִיאַת מִצְרַיִם כָּל־אוֹתוֹ הַלַּיְלָה. עַד־
שֶׁבָּאוּ תַלְמִידֵיהֶם וְאָמְרוּ לָהֶם. רַבּוֹתֵינוּ. הִגִּיעַ זְמַן
קְרִיאַת שְׁמַע שֶׁל־שַׁחֲרִית:

There is a tale about Rabbi Eliezer, Rabbi Yehoshua, Rabbi
Elazar ben Azaria, Rabbi Akiba, and Rabbi Tarfon, who
were gathered in Benei Berak, telling the story about the
Going-out of Mitzrayim that whole night, until their students came and said to them: ''Rabbis, the time has come for
saying the morning Shma.''

Reflections

Friends, I have heard a story about this story. It is said that when the five
rabbis met that night, nineteen hundred years ago, they were stirred by
the story of Passover to talk about how to throw off the tyranny of the
Roman Empire. And they told their students to let them know at once if
the Roman troops came into the neighborhood—to let them know by a
code phrase about the morning prayer. So the story goes that they
planned a rebellion that night. For when we are slaves, we must talk, but
we must do more than talk.

*   *   *   *   *

(In the manner of good rabbinic storytelling, one tale about Rabbi Elazar
ben Azaria suggests another:)

אָמַר רַבִּי אֶלְעָזָר בֶּן־עֲזַרְיָה. הֲרֵי אֲנִי כְּבֶן־שִׁבְעִים שָׁנָה.
וְלֹא זָכִיתִי שֶׁתֵּאָמֵר יְצִיאַת מִצְרַיִם בַּלֵּילוֹת. עַד
שֶׁדְּרָשָׁהּ בֶּן־זוֹמָא. שֶׁנֶּאֱמַר: לְמַעַן תִּזְכֹּר אֶת־יוֹם צֵאתְךָ
מֵאֶרֶץ מִצְרַיִם כֹּל יְמֵי חַיֶּיךָ: יְמֵי חַיֶּיךָ הַיָּמִים. כֹּל יְמֵי
חַיֶּיךָ הַלֵּילוֹת. וַחֲכָמִים אוֹמְרִים יְמֵי חַיֶּיךָ הָעוֹלָם הַזֶּה.
כֹּל יְמֵי חַיֶּיךָ לְהָבִיא לִימוֹת הַמָּשִׁיחַ:

Rabbi Elazar ben Azaria (who was only 18) said: ''I feel as
though I have lived seventy years, but I was never worthy to
understand fully the Biblical basis to include the passage
about the Going-out of Mitzrayim in the evening Shma,

until Ben Zoma found it in the verse, "In order that you may remember your going-out of Mitzrayim all the days of your life" (Deuteronomy 16:3). "The days of your life" suggests just the daytime; "*all* the days of your life" suggests the nights as well.

The sages say that "the days of your life" suggests this world; "all the days of your life" are to bring in the days of the Messiah.

* * * * *

BARUCH HA-MAKOM: Four Praises of God

בָּרוּךְ הַמָּקוֹם.
בָּרוּךְ הוּא.
בָּרוּךְ שֶׁנָּתַן תּוֹרָה לְעַמּוֹ יִשְׂרָאֵל.
בָּרוּךְ הוּא:

Ba-ruch ha-Ma-kom,
Ba-ruch hu.
Ba-ruch she-na-tan To-rah le-a-mo Yis-ra-el,
Ba-ruch hu.

Praised be the One in whom the world finds its true place,
    yet whose place transcends the world.
Praised be the One,
Praised be the One who showed Israel its place by giving
    Your people the Torah,
Praised be the One!

* * * * *

THE FOUR CHILDREN

Reflections: Biblical Sources for the Four Children

1. "And when your children say to you, 'What is this service to you?' (Exodus 12:26) Then you shall say, 'This is the Passover sacrifice to Adonai, who passed over the houses of the children of Israel in Mitzrayim...'" (Exodus 12:27) (This becomes the basis for the *rasha*, the wicked child.)

2. "And you shall tell your child on that day, 'Because of what Adonai did for me when I went out of Mitzrayim.'" (Exodus 13:8) (This becomes the basis for the she-ei-no yo-de-a lish-ol, the child who does not know how to ask.)

3. "And when your child asks you tomorrow, 'What is this?' You shall say, 'With a mighty hand Adonai brought us out of Mitzrayim, out of the house of slaves.'" (Exodus 13:14) (This becomes the basis for the tam, the simple child.)

4. "When your child asks you tomorrow, 'What are the testimonies, the statutes, and the judgments which Adonai our God commanded you?' (Deuteronomy 6:20) Then you shall say to your child, 'We were slaves to Pharaoh in Mitzrayim, and Adonai brought us out of Mitzrayim with a mighty hand.'" (Deuteronomy 6:21) (This becomes the basis for the chacham, the wise child.)

* * * * *

Why should the Torah speak four different times about telling the Exodus story to children? The rabbis (in the midrash to Exodus called the Mechilta [Bo, Parasha 18] say that the passages referred to four different kinds of children—or perhaps to four different qualities that all of us, children and adults, possess. As the Midrash observes after the Four Puzzlements: "In a manner appropriate to the understanding of the child should the parent teach."

* * * * *

כְּנֶגֶד אַרְבָּעָה בָנִים דִּבְּרָה תוֹרָה. אֶחָד חָכָם. וְאֶחָד רָשָׁע. וְאֶחָד תָּם. וְאֶחָד שֶׁאֵינוֹ יוֹדֵעַ לִשְׁאוֹל:

The Torah alludes to four children: one wise (chacham), one wicked (rasha), one simple (tam), and one who does not know what to ask (she-ei-no yo-de-a lish-ol).

חָכָם מַה הוּא אוֹמֵר. מָה הָעֵדֹת וְהַחֻקִּים וְהַמִּשְׁפָּטִים אֲשֶׁר צִוָּה יְיָ אֱלֹהֵינוּ אֶתְכֶם: וְאַף אַתָּה אֱמוֹר לוֹ כְּהִלְכוֹת הַפֶּסַח. אֵין מַפְטִירִין אַחַר הַפֶּסַח אֲפִיקוֹמָן:

What does the Wise One say? "What are the testimonies and the statutes and the judgments which Adonai our God commanded you?" (Deuteronomy 6:20) You should tell this child about the laws of Passover all the way through the section of the Mishnah that says, "One shall not eat any dessert (afikomon) after the paschal lamb," understood in our day to mean, "You shall not eat anything after the afikomon."

רָשָׁע מַה הוּא אוֹמֵר. מָה הָעֲבוֹדָה הַזֹּאת לָכֶם: לָכֶם וְלֹא לוֹ. וּלְפִי שֶׁהוֹצִיא אֶת־עַצְמוֹ מִן־הַכְּלָל כָּפַר בְּעִקָּר. וְאַף אַתָּה הַקְהֵה אֶת־שִׁנָּיו וֶאֱמָר־לוֹ. בַּעֲבוּר זֶה עָשָׂה יְיָ לִי בְּצֵאתִי מִמִּצְרָיִם: לִי וְלֹא לוֹ. אִלּוּ הָיָה שָׁם לֹא הָיָה נִגְאָל:

What does the Wicked One say? "What is this service to you?" To you—but not to her, not to him. And because these Jews remove themselves from the community, they have rejected a major principle of Jewish belief, and so you should set their teeth on edge, discomforting them, by giving them the answer found in Exodus 13:8: "Because of what Adonai did for me when I went out of Mitzrayim." For me and not for them, for had they been there, they would not have been redeemed.

תָּם מַה הוּא אוֹמֵר. מַה־זֹּאת. וְאָמַרְתָּ אֵלָיו. בְּחֹזֶק יָד הוֹצִיאָנוּ יְיָ מִמִּצְרַיִם מִבֵּית עֲבָדִים:

What does the Simple One say? "What is this?" And you should respond with the answer found in Exodus 13:14: "With a mighty hand Adonai brought us out of Mitzrayim, out of the house of slaves."

וְשֶׁאֵינוֹ יוֹדֵעַ לִשְׁאוֹל אַתְּ פְּתַח לוֹ. שֶׁנֶּאֱמַר: וְהִגַּדְתָּ לְבִנְךָ בַּיּוֹם הַהוּא לֵאמֹר. בַּעֲבוּר זֶה עָשָׂה יְיָ לִי בְּצֵאתִי מִמִּצְרָיִם:

And the One Who Does Not Know How to Ask—you must open up for this one, beginning without being asked, as it says in Exodus 13:8: "And you shall tell the story to your child on that day, 'Because of this that Adonai did for me when I went out of Mitzrayim.'"

* * * * *

Perhaps (some Chasidic rabbis suggest) we should turn the order of the Four Children upside down and see the silence of the One Who Does Not Know How to Ask as the most profound response, emerging out of the awesomeness of the Exodus and even of life itself.

If this is so, then (perhaps) the knowledge of the Wise One represents the lowest step on the ladder of learning, which moves from the mastery of facts (*chacham*) to the higher rung of the One Who Is Aware of Separations and Distinctions (*rasha*) to the still higher rung of the One Who Understands Things Simply (*tam*) to the One Whose Understanding Transcends Speech (*she-ei-no yo-de-a lish-ol*). The Haggadah tells us that this is the One to whom we must open up; it is through the Silent One, the one who has moved beyond the questions, through whom we may understand what Adonai really did for each of us when we went out of Mitzrayim.

* * * * *

(Song: "The Ballad of the Four Children," p. 144, might be sung here to the tune of "Clementine.")

A MIDRASHIC DIALOGUE: How the Torah Text Shapes the Haggadah

וְהִגַּדְתָּ לְבִנְךָ. יָכוֹל מֵרֹאשׁ חֹדֶשׁ. תַּלְמוּד לוֹמַר בַּיּוֹם
הַהוּא. אִי בַּיּוֹם הַהוּא יָכוֹל מִבְּעוֹד יוֹם. תַּלְמוּד לוֹמַר
בַּעֲבוּר זֶה. בַּעֲבוּר זֶה לֹא אָמַרְתִּי אֶלָּא בְּשָׁעָה שֶׁיֵּשׁ
מַצָּה וּמָרוֹר מֻנָּחִים לְפָנֶיךָ:

"And you shall tell the story to your child on that day: 'Because of this that Adonai did for me . . .'" (Exodus 13:8, the answer to the child who does not know how to ask).

We might think we should begin to tell the story on the First of Nisan, on Rosh Chodesh, as a preparation for Pesach.

But the text says, "On that day," which must mean: on the very day of Pesach.

All right, if we are to begin only "on that day," we might think we should start the story while it is still day!

But the text also says, "Because of *this*." *This* must mean something we can point to, and so "because of *this*," I cannot start the story until the moment when matzah and maror are set out before us.

Reflections

All things in Jewish life need preparation. We prepare for Shabbat, we must build a sukkah before we eat in it, we study the Passover laws and rid our homes of chametz before the holiday begins—but the essential act of Pesach, telling the story, is not prepared for. It is reserved, like the special taste of matzah, for the Seder night. And as a tribute to the Speechless One, the name of the Seder rite, Haggadah—Telling the Story—comes only from the response to that child: "You shall tell the story (*ve-hi-ga-de-ta*) to your child on that day, because of *this*."

* * * * *

OUR DEGRADATION: Not Slavery (Avadim Hayinu) but Idolatry (Avodah Zarah)

Reflections

The first answer to the Four Puzzlements was the Talmudic sage Shmuel's: we celebrate tonight because our ancestors moved from physical slavery to the ability to tell the story of the Exodus. His opponent in the Talmudic debate, Rav, believed that our original degradation was the idolatry in which Abraham was raised, and that our praise was the promise to Abraham that the generation that was to be enslaved would also be freed.

For Rav, the degradation lies in the spiritual realm (idolatry), but the praise is for physical freedom. For Shmuel, the degradation lies in the physical realm (slavery), but the praise is spiritual—concluding the story of the Exodus with psalms of praise. Both rabbis, therefore, teach the intimate connection between the spiritual subjugation of polytheism and the physical subjugation to which it leads.

מִתְּחִלָּה עוֹבְדֵי עֲבוֹדָה זָרָה הָיוּ אֲבוֹתֵינוּ (וְאִמּוֹתֵינוּ).
וְעַכְשָׁו קֵרְבָנוּ הַמָּקוֹם לַעֲבוֹדָתוֹ. שֶׁנֶּאֱמַר: וַיֹּאמֶר
יְהוֹשֻׁעַ אֶל־כָּל־הָעָם. כֹּה אָמַר יְיָ אֱלֹהֵי יִשְׂרָאֵל בְּעֵבֶר
הַנָּהָר יָשְׁבוּ אֲבוֹתֵיכֶם מֵעוֹלָם תֶּרַח אֲבִי אַבְרָהָם וַאֲבִי
נָחוֹר וַיַּעַבְדוּ אֱלֹהִים אֲחֵרִים: וָאֶקַּח אֶת אֲבִיכֶם אֶת־

אַבְרָהָם מֵעֵבֶר הַנָּהָר. וָאוֹלֵךְ אוֹתוֹ בְּכָל־אֶרֶץ כְּנָעַן
וָאַרְבֶּה אֶת־זַרְעוֹ וָאֶתֶּן־לוֹ אֶת־יִצְחָק: וָאֶתֵּן לְיִצְחָק
אֶת־יַעֲקֹב וְאֶת־עֵשָׂו. וָאֶתֵּן לְעֵשָׂו אֶת־הַר שֵׂעִיר לָרֶשֶׁת
אוֹתוֹ וְיַעֲקֹב וּבָנָיו יָרְדוּ מִצְרָיִם:

From the beginning our ancestors served many gods. But now the Omnipresent has brought us near to the service of the One. As the Bible tells us: "And Joshua spoke to all the people: 'Thus said Adonai, God of Israel: "On the other side of the river dwelt our ancestors, from the beginning of the world—Terach the father of Abraham and the father of Nachor. They served other gods.

"But I took your father Abraham and your mother Sarah away from the other side of the river, and I led them throughout the land of Canaan, multiplying their seed. I gave them Isaac, to Isaac and Rebecca I gave Jacob and Esau, and I gave Esau Mount Seir to inherit. But Jacob and his sons went down to Mitzrayim."'" (Joshua 24:2–4)

Reflections

The Mechilta, the Midrash to Exodus, asks why the Torah refers to polytheism as the worship of "other gods," *elohim acherim.* Can there really be any "other" gods?

One person answered: Because they are the objects other peoples (*acherim*) call gods.

Someone else responded: Because they bring other things than good into the world and so delay (*me-ach-rim*) the coming of goodness.

A third person said: Because they have no real power, serving them makes their worshippers "other," alien (*acherim*) from the true Source of power and from their own inner power which the Source has given them.

A final interpretation: Because they act like "others," aliens (*acherim*), to their worshippers, since they have no capacity for relationship with those who serve them.

And we might add: It is said that we today also serve "other gods." Do you agree? What are they, and how do we serve them? Do the "other gods" we serve have the effects on us which the Mechilta describes?

GOD'S PROMISE

בָּרוּךְ שׁוֹמֵר הַבְטָחָתוֹ לְיִשְׂרָאֵל. בָּרוּךְ הוּא. שֶׁהַקָּדוֹשׁ
בָּרוּךְ הוּא חִשֵּׁב אֶת־הַקֵּץ לַעֲשׂוֹת כְּמָה שֶׁאָמַר
לְאַבְרָהָם אָבִינוּ בִּבְרִית בֵּין הַבְּתָרִים. שֶׁנֶּאֱמַר: וַיֹּאמֶר
לְאַבְרָם יָדֹעַ תֵּדַע כִּי־גֵר יִהְיֶה זַרְעֲךָ בְּאֶרֶץ לֹא לָהֶם
וַעֲבָדוּם וְעִנּוּ אֹתָם אַרְבַּע מֵאוֹת שָׁנָה: וְגַם אֶת־הַגּוֹי
אֲשֶׁר יַעֲבֹדוּ דָּן אָנֹכִי. וְאַחֲרֵי־כֵן יֵצְאוּ בִּרְכֻשׁ גָּדוֹל:

Praised are You who keeps Your promise to Israel; we praise
You! For the *Kadosh-baruch-hu*, the Blessed Holy One, calculated the end of their captivity, in order to fulfill what God
had promised to Abraham our Father in the Covenant
Between the Pieces (Genesis 15:13–14):

"And God said to Avram, 'Know for certain that your seed
will be a stranger in a land that is not theirs, and they will
serve them and suffer their oppression for 400 years. But
then the nation which they have served shall I judge, and
afterwards they shall come out with great substance.'"

Reflections

We are about to cover the matzot and raise a cup of wine, acknowledging
the eternal saving presence of God by offering the *Ve-hi she-am-da*
below. This is similar to the Shabbat custom of keeping the challot
covered while wine is raised for Kiddush in acknowledgment of God's
gift of the seventh day.

For we do not wish to slight the challot and matzah, representing God's
miraculous gift of manna. Rather we cover them, so that the gift represented by the wine and the gift represented by the bread can each be
considered separately, as a separate cause for thanksgiving to God.

DIRECTIONS: Cover the matzot and raise a cup of wine.

VE-HI SHE-AM-DA

וְהִיא שֶׁעָמְדָה לַאֲבוֹתֵינוּ [וּלְאִמוֹתֵינוּ] וְלָנוּ. שֶׁלֹא אֶחָד
בִּלְבַד עָמַד עָלֵינוּ לְכַלוֹתֵנוּ. אֶלָּא שֶׁבְּכָל־דּוֹר וָדוֹר
עוֹמְדִים עָלֵינוּ לְכַלוֹתֵנוּ. וְהַקָּדוֹשׁ בָּרוּךְ הוּא מַצִּילֵנוּ
מִיָּדָם:

Ve-hi she-am-da la-a-vo-tei-nu [u-le-i-mo-tei-nu] ve-
la-nu, she-lo e-chad bi-le-vad a-mad a-lei-nu le-cha-lo-
tei-nu, eh-la she-be-chol dor va-dor o-me-dim a-lei-nu
le-cha-lo-tei-nu, ve-ha-ka-dosh ba-ruch-hu ma-tzi-lei-
nu mi-ya-dam.

This promise has stood fast for our fathers, for our mothers,
and for us:
For not just one person has stood against us to destroy us,
But in every single generation there are those who stand
against us to destroy us,
Yet the Kadosh-baruch-hu, the Blessed Holy One, keeps
saving us from their hand!

DIRECTIONS: Set down the wine cup and uncover the matzot for the con-
tinuation of their story.

Reflections

On God's Promise

In the same chapter in which God promised Abraham that his and
Sarah's seed would be slaves for 400 years (Genesis 15:13 f., see p. 36),
God also promised that their seed would one day be as numerous as the
stars in heaven, and that their seed would one day inherit the Land of
Israel. As we saw in the midrash to the Song of Songs (p. 21), the rabbis
calculated that God freed the Israelites after 210 years of slavery—an act
of mercy, they believed.

And the promises to Abraham are on their way to coming true. We have
suffered greatly, but we have also become a people of some numbers
around the world, and we have a stronger claim to the Land of Israel
than we have had in 2000 years. Though our suffering continues, God
has not yet failed to "keep saving us from their hand."

* * * * *

As it is customary, the rabbi began to explain the meaning of Passover in response to the Four Questions. But on that Seder night in Bergen Belsen, the ancient questions of the Haggadah assumed a unique meaning.

"Night," said the rabbi, "means exile, darkness, suffering. Morning means light, hope, redemption. Why is this night different from all other nights? Why is this suffering, the Holocaust, different from all the previous sufferings of the Jewish people?" No one attempted to respond to the rabbi's questions. Rabbi Israel Spira continued.

"For on all other nights we eat either bread or matzah, but tonight only matzah. Bread is leavened; it has height. Matzah is unleavened and is totally flat. During all our previous sufferings, during all our previous nights in exile, we Jews had bread and matzah. We had moments of bread, of creativity and light, and moments of matzah, of suffering and despair. But tonight, the night of the Holocaust, we experience our greatest suffering. But do not despair, my young friends."

The rabbi continued in a forceful voice filled with faith. "For this is also the beginning of our redemption. We are slaves who served Pharaoh in Egypt. Slaves in Hebrew are *avadim*; the Hebrew letters of the word *avadim* form an acronym for the Hebrew phrase: David, the son of Jesse, your servant, your Messiah. Thus, even in our state of slavery we find intimations of our eventual freedom through the coming of the Messiah.

"We who are witnessing the darkest night in history, the lowest moment of civilization, will also witness the great light of redemption, for before the great light there will be a long night, as was promised by our Prophets. 'But it shall come to pass, that at evening there shall be light,' and 'The people that walked in darkness have seen a great light; they that dwelt in the land of the shadow of death, upon them hath the light shined.' It was to us, my dear children, that our prophets have spoken, to us who dwell in the shadow of death, to us who will live to witness the great light of redemption."

TZEI U-LE-MAD: Redemption Through Study

(An alternative to this section may be found beginning on p. 49)

Reflections

The story is told (Shabbat 31a) that Hillel the Elder was once approached by a worshipper of idols and asked to explain the whole Torah while the man was standing on one foot. Understanding that the pagan's question provided an opportunity to demonstrate the patience, humor, and wisdom that can be acquired through Torah study, Hillel replied, "What is hateful to you do not do to your neighbor. That is the whole Torah, the rest is commentary. Now go and study."

"Go and study," *tzei u-le-mad*, is the name the Haggadah gives to this section of interplay between a short Biblical passage, Deuteronomy 26:5–8, and the rabbinic commentary which follows it (taken from the midrashic collection called Sifrei, section Ki Tavo, Piska 301.)

The written Torah, the rabbis held, consists merely of chapter headings: each phrase, each word, points to hidden meanings which Moses was able only to hint at in the way he wrote down the Torah God was dictating to him. It was left for later generations of serious probers to uncover the hints which Moses' text provided.

In raising and answering questions on the Haggadah, we have been composing our own midrash tonight, uncovering some of the meanings Moses knew were hidden away, like the afikomon, waiting for us to find this very night. Now let us take a little time to wrestle with the Haggadah's midrash to a remarkably concise history of Israel, from Jacob's descent into Mitzrayim to his grandchildren's emergence into freedom. That history is found in these four verses from Deuteronomy that all Israelites were expected to offer to God whenever they brought a basket of first fruits to the Temple altar.

DEUTERONOMY 26:5–8

אֲרַמִּי אֹבֵד אָבִי וַיֵּרֶד מִצְרַיְמָה וַיָּגָר שָׁם בִּמְתֵי מְעָט.
וַיְהִי־שָׁם לְגוֹי גָּדוֹל עָצוּם וָרָב: וַיָּרֵעוּ אֹתָנוּ הַמִּצְרִים
וַיְעַנּוּנוּ. וַיִּתְּנוּ עָלֵינוּ עֲבֹדָה קָשָׁה: וַנִּצְעַק אֶל־יְיָ אֱלֹהֵי
אֲבֹתֵינוּ. וַיִּשְׁמַע יְיָ אֶת־קֹלֵנוּ וַיַּרְא אֶת־עָנְיֵנוּ וְאֶת־
עֲמָלֵנוּ וְאֶת־לַחֲצֵנוּ: וַיּוֹצִאֵנוּ יְיָ מִמִּצְרַיִם בְּיָד חֲזָקָה
וּבִזְרֹעַ נְטוּיָה וּבְמֹרָא גָּדֹל. וּבְאֹתוֹת וּבְמֹפְתִים:

A wandering Aramean was my father, who went down to Mitzrayim and sojourned there, few in number. And there we became a great nation, strong and numerous. But the Egyptians dealt ill with us and afflicted us, setting hard labor upon us. Yet when we cried out to Adonai, the God of our ancestors, Adonai heard our voice, seeing our affliction, our toil, and our oppression. *Then Adonai brought us out from Mitzrayim with a strong hand and an outstretched arm; with great awe, with signs, and with wonders.*

צֵא וּלְמַד מַה־בִּקֵּשׁ לָבָן הָאֲרַמִּי לַעֲשׂוֹת לְיַעֲקֹב אָבִינוּ. שֶׁפַּרְעֹה לֹא גָזַר אֶלָּא עַל־הַזְּכָרִים. וְלָבָן בִּקֵּשׁ לַעֲקוֹר אֶת־הַכֹּל.

Go forth and learn (*tzei u-le-mad*) what Laban the Aramean sought to do to Jacob our father: Pharaoh decreed death only for the males, while Laban sought to uproot us all.

VERSE 5

שֶׁנֶּאֱמַר: אֲרַמִּי אֹבֵד אָבִי וַיֵּרֶד מִצְרַיְמָה וַיָּגָר שָׁם בִּמְתֵי מְעָט. וַיְהִי־שָׁם לְגוֹי גָּדוֹל עָצוּם וָרָב:

For it is said: "A wandering Aramean was my father, who went down to Mitzrayim and sojourned there, few in number. And there we became a great nation, strong and numerous."

Reflections

The written text seems to refer to Jacob, who lived in Aram, in Mesopotamia, while he was courting Rachel and Leah and working for their father Laban. But the midrash says if you change the vowels (from *oved*, "wandering," to *ibed*, "destroyed"), "A wandering Aramean was my father" will read, "An Aramean tried to destroy my father," reminding us of the treachery of Laban, who tricked Jacob into marrying Leah before Rachel, tricked him into twenty years of servitude, and finally tried to deny him his dowry. Laban is the symbol of everyone who has forced the Jews to live by our wits instead of our faith.

Thus we translate with the midrash: "An Aramean tried to destroy my father. But he went down to Mitzrayim and sojourned there, few in number, yet there he became a great nation, strong and numerous."

וַיֵּרֶד מִצְרַיְמָה. אָנוּס עַל־פִּי הַדִּבּוּר:

But he went down to Mitzrayim: Impelled by the word of God's promise to Abraham.

Reflections

Jacob sensed he was an instrument of God's design, and so agreed to descend into Mitzrayim, the narrow place, to help fulfill the promise of his people's ascent into the open spaces of the Land of Promise.

וַיָּגָר שָׁם. מְלַמֵּד שֶׁלֹּא יָרַד יַעֲקֹב לְהִשְׁתַּקֵּעַ בְּמִצְרַיִם
אֶלָּא לָגוּר שָׁם. שֶׁנֶּאֱמַר: וַיֹּאמְרוּ אֶל־פַּרְעֹה לָגוּר בָּאָרֶץ
בָּאנוּ כִּי־אֵין מִרְעֶה לַצֹּאן אֲשֶׁר לַעֲבָדֶיךָ כִּי־כָבֵד הָרָעָב
בְּאֶרֶץ כְּנָעַן. וְעַתָּה יֵשְׁבוּ־נָא עֲבָדֶיךָ בְּאֶרֶץ גֹּשֶׁן:

And sojourned there: This emphasizes that our ancestor Jacob never planned to sink roots there, but only to stay for a while, as it is said: "And Joseph's brothers said to Pharaoh, 'Only to sojourn in the land have we come, for there is no food for our flocks in the Land of Canaan.'" (Genesis 47:4)

בִּמְתֵי מְעָט. כְּמָה שֶׁנֶּאֱמַר: בְּשִׁבְעִים נֶפֶשׁ יָרְדוּ אֲבֹתֶיךָ
מִצְרָיְמָה. וְעַתָּה שָׂמְךָ יְיָ אֱלֹהֶיךָ כְּכוֹכְבֵי הַשָּׁמַיִם לָרֹב:

Few in number: As it is said: "As a band of seventy persons our ancestors went down to Mitzrayim, and now Adonai your God has made your numbers as great as the stars in heaven!" (Deuteronomy 10:22)

Reflections

The growth in numbers from the 70 who entered to the 600,000 and more who left has classically been seen as proof of God's faithfulness to the promise made to Abraham. Still, so long as we can count our numbers, God's promise that we would be as uncountable as the stars has not yet been fulfilled. In that sense, no matter how many Jews participate in Jewish life—in Hillel, in synagogues, centers, and organizations, as contributors to UJA/Federation campaigns—there are Jews who will never be satisfied till our number becomes too great for anyone to count.

וַיְהִי־שָׁם לְגוֹי. מְלַמֵּד שֶׁהָיוּ יִשְׂרָאֵל מְצֻיָּנִים שָׁם:

And became a nation there: This indicates that even in Mitzrayim, Israel was distinguished as a nation, maintaining

(according to the rabbis) their names, their language, and
their morality.

גָּדוֹל עָצוּם. כְּמָה שֶׁנֶּאֱמַר. וּבְנֵי יִשְׂרָאֵל פָּרוּ וַיִּשְׁרְצוּ
וַיִּרְבּוּ וַיַּעַצְמוּ בִּמְאֹד מְאֹד. וַתִּמָּלֵא הָאָרֶץ אֹתָם:

Great, mighty: As it is said: "And the children of Israel were
fruitful and spread abroad, mightily increasing to a great
degree, so that the land was filled with them." (Exodus 1:7)

וָרָב. כְּמָה שֶׁנֶּאֱמַר: רְבָבָה כְּצֶמַח הַשָּׂדֶה נְתַתִּיךְ וַתִּרְבִּי
וַתִּגְדְּלִי וַתָּבֹאִי בַּעֲדִי עֲדָיִים. שָׁדַיִם נָכֹנוּ וּשְׂעָרֵךְ צִמֵּחַ
וְאַתְּ עֵרֹם וְעֶרְיָה: וָאֶעֱבֹר עָלַיִךְ וָאֶרְאֵךְ מִתְבּוֹסֶסֶת
בְּדָמָיִךְ וָאֹמַר לָךְ בְּדָמַיִךְ חֲיִי וָאֹמַר לָךְ בְּדָמַיִךְ חֲיִי:

And numerous: As it is said (Ezekiel 16:7,6): "I have given
you myriads, like shoots from the field, and you became
numerous and great, you came to be beautiful, adorned;
your breasts grew firm, your hair luxuriant, yet you were
still naked and bare. And I passed by you and saw you wal-
lowing in your blood (literally, *"in your bloods"*); I said to
you, "Through your blood (literally, *"through your
bloods"*) you shall live; through your blood you shall live."

Reflections

Once more, as in the Song of Songs, Israel is portrayed as the lover of
God, splendid yet bare—which the rabbis understood to mean bare of
mitzvot when God found us in Mitzrayim, before the Torah was given.
To "clothe" us, to make us "respectable" for the Exodus wedding
journey with God, the Blessed Holy One gave us in Mitzrayim two
mitzvot: *brit milah* (circumcizing our sons) and putting the blood of the
Pesach lamb on the doorpost. Both mitzvot involve the flow of blood,
which is how the rabbis interpret the plural "bloods" in the Ezekiel
verse. By giving us these two mitzvot of "national distinctiveness," God
has helped keep the promise to Abraham that we would survive—hence,
"through your bloods you shall live."

VERSE 6

וַיָּרֵעוּ אֹתָנוּ הַמִּצְרִים וַיְעַנּוּנוּ. וַיִּתְּנוּ עָלֵינוּ עֲבֹדָה קָשָׁה:

And the Egyptians dealt wickedly with us and afflicted us, imposing upon us hard service.

וַיָּרֵעוּ אֹתָנוּ הַמִּצְרִים. כְּמָה שֶׁנֶּאֱמַר: הָבָה נִתְחַכְּמָה לוֹ. פֶּן־יִרְבֶּה וְהָיָה כִּי־תִקְרֶאנָה מִלְחָמָה וְנוֹסַף גַּם־הוּא עַל־שֹׂנְאֵינוּ וְנִלְחַם־בָּנוּ וְעָלָה מִן־הָאָרֶץ:

And the Egyptians dealt wickedly with us: As it is said: "Come, let us deal shrewdly with this nation lest it multiply, and should war break out it might even join itself to our enemies and fight against us, and then go up out of the land." (Exodus 1:10)

וַיְעַנּוּנוּ. כְּמָה שֶׁנֶּאֱמַר: וַיָּשִׂימוּ עָלָיו שָׂרֵי מִסִּים לְמַעַן עַנֹּתוֹ בְּסִבְלֹתָם. וַיִּבֶן עָרֵי מִסְכְּנוֹת לְפַרְעֹה אֶת־פִּתֹם וְאֶת־רַעַמְסֵס:

And they afflicted us: As it is said: "And they set upon this nation taskmasters to afflict it through their burdens. And it built storecities for Pharaoh—Pitom and Raamses." (Exodus 1:11)

Reflections

The Egyptians speak of Israel here always as a collective, not as individuals. We, too, often speak of those we don't know well as though they were all alike—*the* Gentiles, *the* disabled, *the* Palestinians, *the* Blacks. We would like to think that if the Egyptians had known each of us here tonight, they would never have seen us as aliens, nor would they have been able to afflict us so. It is an ominous reminder of the dangers inherent in ignoring the ways in which members of a group really are alike: in their individuality, and their divinely created humanity.

וַיִּתְּנוּ עָלֵינוּ עֲבֹדָה קָשָׁה. כְּמָה שֶׁנֶּאֱמַר: וַיַּעֲבִדוּ מִצְרַיִם אֶת־בְּנֵי יִשְׂרָאֵל בְּפָרֶךְ:

They imposed hard service upon us. As it is said: "And Egyptians made the Israelites serve with rigor." (Exodus 1:13)

Reflections

Several commentators have noted that this verse demonstrates that not only Pharaoh's officers but *ordinary Egyptians* imposed slavery on Israel, and thus the punishments they suffered through plagues and the drowning at the Reed Sea were not the punishments of innocents but of parties who directly shared in Pharaoh's guilt. Abraham Joshua Heschel once said, "In a free society, some are guilty; all are responsible."

VERSE 7

וַנִּצְעַק אֶל־יְיָ אֱלֹהֵי אֲבֹתֵינוּ. וַיִּשְׁמַע יְיָ אֶת־קֹלֵנוּ וַיַּרְא אֶת־עָנְיֵנוּ וְאֶת־עֲמָלֵנוּ וְאֶת־לַחֲצֵנוּ:

But when we cried out to Adonai, the God of our ancestors, Adonai heard our voice, seeing our affliction and our toil and our oppression.

וַנִּצְעַק אֶל־יְיָ אֱלֹהֵי אֲבֹתֵינוּ. כְּמָה שֶׁנֶּאֱמַר: וַיְהִי בַיָּמִים הָרַבִּים הָהֵם וַיָּמָת מֶלֶךְ מִצְרַיִם וַיֵּאָנְחוּ בְנֵי־יִשְׂרָאֵל מִן־הָעֲבֹדָה וַיִּזְעָקוּ. וַתַּעַל שַׁוְעָתָם אֶל־הָאֱלֹהִים מִן־הָעֲבֹדָה:

But when we cried out to Adonai, God of our ancestors. As it is written: "And in the course of those many days, the king of Mitzrayim died, and the Israelites sighed from servitude and cried out. And their cry went up to God from their servitude." (Exodus 2:23)

וַיִּשְׁמַע יְיָ אֶת־קֹלֵנוּ. כְּמָה שֶׁנֶּאֱמַר: וַיִּשְׁמַע אֱלֹהִים אֶת־נַאֲקָתָם. וַיִּזְכֹּר אֱלֹהִים אֶת־בְּרִיתוֹ אֶת־אַבְרָהָם אֶת־יִצְחָק וְאֶת־יַעֲקֹב:

And Adonai heard our voice. As it is written: "And God heard their groaning, and God remembered the covenant with Abraham, with Isaac, and with Jacob." (Exodus 22:4)

וַיַּרְא אֶת־עָנְיֵנוּ. זוֹ פְּרִישׁוּת דֶּרֶךְ אֶרֶץ. כְּמָה שֶׁנֶּאֱמַר:
וַיַּרְא אֱלֹהִים אֶת־בְּנֵי יִשְׂרָאֵל. וַיֵּדַע אֱלֹהִים:

Seeing our affliction. This refers to the Egyptian prohibition against the Israelites' making love, as it is said: "And when God beheld the Israelites, God knew." (Exodus 2:25)

Reflections

It is telling that Pharaoh's prohibition of lovemaking was the affliction that finally gave God the "knowledge" of the seriousness of Israel's plight. What else God "knew" is the subject of some rabbinic speculation.

Another response: However much the Israelites might rebel against God on their way out of Egypt, *God knew* that they would ultimately affirm the divine existence, as they did at the splitting of the Sea: "This is my God, whom I shall glorify!"

However the Israelites might later worship the Golden Calf, *God knew* that ultimately they would cry out, "*Na-a-seh ve-nish-ma*, we shall do and we shall understand," agreeing to do God's will even before they understood it.

וְאֶת־עֲמָלֵנוּ. אֵלּוּ הַבָּנִים. כְּמָה שֶׁנֶּאֱמַר: כָּל־הַבֵּן הַיִּלּוֹד
הַיְאֹרָה תַּשְׁלִיכֻהוּ. וְכָל־הַבַּת תְּחַיּוּן:

And our toil: This refers to our sons, as it is said: "Every son that is born you shall cast into the river, while every daughter you shall keep alive." (Exodus 1:22)

וְאֶת־לַחֲצֵנוּ. זֶה הַדֹּחַק. כְּמָה שֶׁנֶּאֱמַר: וְגַם־רָאִיתִי
אֶת־הַלַּחַץ אֲשֶׁר מִצְרַיִם לֹחֲצִים אֹתָם:

And our oppression: This refers to the force applied against them, as it is said: "And I have also seen the force with which the Egyptians have forced themselves on them." (Exodus 3:9)

וַיּוֹצִאֵנוּ יְיָ מִמִּצְרַיִם בְּיָד חֲזָקָה וּבִזְרֹעַ נְטוּיָה וּבְמֹרָא
גָּדֹל. וּבְאֹתוֹת וּבְמֹפְתִים:

*But Adonai brought us out of Mitzrayim with a mighty hand
and an outstretched arm, with great awe, and with signs and
wonders.*

וַיּוֹצִאֵנוּ יְיָ מִמִּצְרַיִם. לֹא־עַל־יְדֵי מַלְאָךְ. וְלֹא־עַל־יְדֵי
שָׂרָף. וְלֹא־עַל־יְדֵי שָׁלִיחַ. אֶלָּא הַקָּדוֹשׁ בָּרוּךְ הוּא
בִּכְבוֹדוֹ וּבְעַצְמוֹ. שֶׁנֶּאֱמַר: וְעָבַרְתִּי בְאֶרֶץ־מִצְרַיִם
בַּלַּיְלָה הַזֶּה וְהִכֵּיתִי כָל־בְּכוֹר בְּאֶרֶץ מִצְרַיִם מֵאָדָם
וְעַד־בְּהֵמָה. וּבְכָל־אֱלֹהֵי מִצְרַיִם אֶעֱשֶׂה שְׁפָטִים אֲנִי יְיָ:

But Adonai brought us out of Mitzrayim: Not through an
angel, not through a fiery seraph, not through an emissary,
but the Blessed Holy One alone in glory and in might. As it is
said: "And as I pass through the land of Mitzrayim in that
night, I shall smite every first-born in the land of Mitzrayim,
from the highest born human being to the lowliest creature.
And against all the gods of Mitzrayim shall I bring
judgments, I Adonai!" (Exodus 12:12)

(Why does the text from Exodus 12:12 use the word "I" so
often? The midrash reads it this way:)

וְעָבַרְתִּי בְאֶרֶץ־מִצְרַיִם בַּלַּיְלָה הַזֶּה. אֲנִי וְלֹא מַלְאָךְ.
וְהִכֵּיתִי כָל־בְּכוֹר בְּאֶרֶץ מִצְרַיִם. אֲנִי וְלֹא שָׂרָף. וּבְכָל־
אֱלֹהֵי מִצְרַיִם אֶעֱשֶׂה שְׁפָטִים. אֲנִי וְלֹא שָׁלִיחַ. אֲנִי הוּא
וְלֹא אַחֵר:

*And as I pass through the land of Mitzrayim in that night—I
and not an angel, I shall smite every first-born in the land of
Mitzrayim—I and not a seraph; and against all the gods of
Mitzrayim shall I bring judgments—I and not an emissary, I,
Adonai—I and no other!*

For many modern Jews who often do not take angels or seraphim—angels in flames—very seriously, to deny their role in the Exodus is to state the obvious. But in their place we often put other "emissaries"—human agents, the forces of history, even co-operating natural phenomena. But the Haggadah insists that we should praise only God for the redemption. It might say the same for Israel's War of Independence, the Six-Day War, and other struggles: the generals, the politicians, the people were all the instruments of God's design, not the ultimate causes of the victory.

* * * * *

בְּיָד חֲזָקָה. זוּ הַדֶּבֶר. כְּמָה שֶׁנֶּאֱמַר: הִנֵּה יַד־יְיָ הוֹיָה
בְּמִקְנְךָ אֲשֶׁר בַּשָּׂדֶה בַּסּוּסִים בַּחֲמֹרִים בַּגְּמַלִּים בַּבָּקָר
וּבַצֹּאן. דֶּבֶר כָּבֵד מְאֹד:

With a mighty hand: This refers to the cattle plague, as it is said: "Behold, the hand of Adonai is against the cattle in the field, horses and donkeys, camels, herds and flocks, a heavy plague indeed." (Exodus 9:3)

וּבִזְרֹעַ נְטוּיָה. זוּ הַחֶרֶב. כְּמָה שֶׁנֶּאֱמַר: וְחַרְבּוֹ שְׁלוּפָה
בְּיָדוֹ נְטוּיָה עַל־יְרוּשָׁלָיִם:

And an outstretched arm: This refers to the sword, as it is said: "And a drawn sword in his hand outstretched over Jerusalem." (I Chronicles 21:16)

וּבְמֹרָא גָּדֹל. זֶה גִּלּוּי שְׁכִינָה. כְּמָה שֶׁנֶּאֱמַר: אוֹ הֲנִסָּה
אֱלֹהִים לָבוֹא לָקַחַת לוֹ גוֹי מִקֶּרֶב גּוֹי בְּמַסֹּת בְּאֹתֹת
וּבְמוֹפְתִים וּבְמִלְחָמָה וּבְיָד חֲזָקָה וּבִזְרוֹעַ נְטוּיָה
וּבְמוֹרָאִים גְּדֹלִים. כְּכֹל אֲשֶׁר־עָשָׂה לָכֶם יְיָ אֱלֹהֵיכֶם
בְּמִצְרַיִם לְעֵינֶיךָ:

With great awe: This refers to the appearance of the Shechina, when the Israelites beheld the presence of God, as it is said: "Or has God tried to come and take in a nation from amidst another nation through tasks and trials, signs, wonders, and war, with a mighty hand and an outstretched arm and great feats of awe, such as Adonai your God did for you in Mitzrayim before your very eyes?" (Deuteronomy 4:34)

Reflections

God entered the consciousness of the Israelites gradually: first the divine "hand" was shown through plagues directed against the animals, farms, and rivers of the Egyptians, allowing some to believe they were merely natural phenomena—as some in our own day still understand the plagues. Then God appeared through the "sword"—the slaying of the first-born—more terrifying, surely, yet still, it could be argued, a natural phenomenon. Finally God appeared at the Sea as Shechina, the Divine Presence itself. This appearance is described only through the people's reaction: "great awe"—not only as death now, but even more as life, and liberation.

We are unlikely in our time to behold a sea splitting in two, but when we feel "great awe," when we feel surrounded by exultant life, when we feel a sudden rush of liberation—these can be signs that the Divine Presence is appearing to us as well.

וּבְאֹתוֹת. זֶה הַמַּטֶּה. כְּמָה שֶׁנֶּאֱמַר: וְאֶת־הַמַּטֶּה הַזֶּה תִּקַּח בְּיָדֶךָ. אֲשֶׁר תַּעֲשֶׂה־בּוֹ אֶת־הָאֹתֹת:

And with signs: This refers to the staff, as it is said (Exodus 4:17, God speaking to Moses): "And take this staff in your hand, that you may do the signs with it."

וּבְמֹפְתִים. זֶה הַדָּם. כְּמָה שֶׁנֶּאֱמַר: וְנָתַתִּי מוֹפְתִים בַּשָּׁמַיִם וּבָאָרֶץ. דָּם וָאֵשׁ וְתִימְרוֹת עָשָׁן:

And wonders: This refers to the blood, as it is said: "And I shall put wonders in heaven and earth: blood and fire and pillars of smoke!" (Joel 3:3)

דָּבָר אַחֵר.

בְּיָד חֲזָקָה שְׁתַּיִם. וּבִזְרֹעַ נְטוּיָה שְׁתַּיִם. וּבְמֹרָא גָדֹל שְׁתַּיִם. וּבְאֹתוֹת שְׁתַּיִם. וּבְמֹפְתִים שְׁתַּיִם:

Another explanation:

Mighty hand is two words
Outstretched arm is two words
Great awe is two words
Signs is a plural, meaning at least two
Wonders is a plural, meaning at least two

These add up to ten, signifying the ten plagues which the Blessed Holy One brought upon the Egyptians in Mitzrayim.

(Continue with The Ten Plagues on p. 51)

* * * * *

AN ALTERNATIVE TZEI U-LE-MAD: The Torah Tells the Story (Exodus 1:6–3:20)

1:6   Now Yosef died, and all his brothers, and all that generation.

7   Yet the children of Israel bore fruit, they swarmed, they became many, they grew powerful—exceedingly, yes, exceedingly;
the land filled up with them.

8   Now a new king arose over Egypt, who had not known Yosef.

9   He said to his people:
Here, (this) people, the Children of Israel, is many more numerous and powerful than we!

10   Come now, let us use our wits against it,
lest it become many more,
and then, if war should occur,
it too be added to our enemies
and make war upon us
or go up away from the land!

11   So they set gang-captains over it, to afflict it with their burdens.
It built storage-cities for Pharaoh—Pitom and Ra'amses.

12   But as they afflicted it, so did it become many, so did it burst forth.
And they felt dread before the Children of Israel.

13 So they, Egypt, made the Children of Israel subservient
with crushing labor;

14 They embittered their lives with hard servitude in loam
and in bricks and with all kinds of servitude in the
field—

all their service in which they made them subservient with
crushing labor.

15 Now the king of Egypt said to the midwives of the
Hebrews—the name of the first one was Shifra, the
name of the second was Pua—

16 He said:
When you help the Hebrew women give birth, see the
supporting-stones:

if he be a son, put him to death,
but if she be a daughter, she may live.

17 But the midwives feared God,
and they did not do as the king of Egypt had spoken to
them,

they let the (male) children live.
God dealt well with the midwives.
And the people became many and grew exceedingly
powerful.

22 Now Pharaoh commanded all his people, saying:
Every son that is born, throw him into the Nile,
but let every daughter live.

2:23 It was, many years later,
the king of Egypt died.
The Children of Israel groaned from the servitude,
and they cried out;
And their plea for help went up to God, from the servitude.

24 God hearkened to their moaning,
God called to mind the covenant with Avraham, with
Yitzchak, and with Yaakov,

25 God saw the Children of Israel,
God knew.

3:7 Now God said:
I have seen, yes, seen the affliction of my people that is in
Egypt,

their cry have I heard in the face of their slave-drivers;
indeed, I have known their sufferings!

8   So I have come down
to rescue it from the hand of Egypt,
to bring it up from that land
to a land, goodly and spacious,
to a land flowing with milk and honey.
to the place of the Canaanite and the Hittite,
of the Amorite and the Perizzite,
of the Hivvite and the Yevusite.

19   But I, I know
that the king of Egypt will not give you leave to go,
not (even) under a strong hand
20   So I will send forth my hand
and I will strike Egypt with all my wonders which I will do
in its midst—
after that he will send you free!

* * * * *

THE TEN PLAGUES

Reflections

Despite the Torah's suggestion that all the Egyptians participated in our
enslavement and thus deserved punishment, we do not savor their suffering. The Talmud (Megillah 10b) tells us that as the Egyptians were
flailing about in the sea, the angels wanted to sing Halleluyah for Israel's
redemption, but God rebuked them: "How can you sing My praises
when My children are drowning?!"

The Book of Proverbs cautions us: "Do not rejoice when your enemy
falls." (24:17) We reduce the jubilation we might have felt over our
rescue by removing from our cup of joyous wine a drop of joy untasted
for each plague suffered by our oppressors.

DIRECTIONS: As each plague is read by the leader or guests, each person should
remove a drop of wine with finger or spoon and place it on a napkin or plate.

אֵלּוּ עֶשֶׂר מַכּוֹת שֶׁהֵבִיא הַקָּדוֹשׁ בָּרוּךְ הוּא עַל־
הַמִּצְרִים בְּמִצְרַיִם. וְאֵלּוּ הֵן:

E-lu e-ser ma-kot she-he-vi ha-ka-dosh ba-ruch-hu al
ha-mitz-rim be-mitz-ra-yim, ve-e-lu hen:

These ten plagues, which the Blessed Holy One brought
upon the Egyptians in Mitzrayim, are as follows:

3) כִּנִּים.	2) צְפַרְדֵּעַ.	1) דָּם.
Ki-nim	Tze-far-de-a	Dam
Lice	Frogs	Blood

6) שְׁחִין.	5) דֶּבֶר.	4) עָרוֹב.
She-chin	De-ver	A-rov
Boils	Cattle plague	Beasts

9) חֹשֶׁךְ.	8) אַרְבֶּה.	7) בָּרָד.
Cho-shech	Ar-beh	Ba-rad
Darkness	Locusts	Hail

10) מַכַּת־בְּכוֹרוֹת:

Ma-kat Be-cho-rot
Slaying of the
First-Born

רַבִּי יְהוּדָה הָיָה נוֹתֵן בָּהֶם סִמָּנִים.

To help us remember their order, Rabbi Yehudah used to
abbreviate the plagues thus:

3) בְּאַחַ"ב:	2) עֲדַ"שׁ.	1) דְּצַ"ךְ.
Be-ach-av	A-dash	De-tzach

Reflections

Rabbi Yehudah's arrangement reminds us—said the Maharal of Prague,
the great Rabbi Judah Loewe—that the plagues may be understood in
three groups. Blood, frogs, and lice all attacked the Egyptians from
below. The second group, Beasts, Pestilence, and Boils, attacked the
Egyptians on their own level. The third group, Hail, Locusts, and Darkness, attacked the Egyptians from the heavens above. Thus, all Creation
was turned against the Egyptians, while in the Slaying of the First-Born,
listed alone, it is God alone who seals the destruction of Mitzrayim.

* * * * *

Plagues in Our Mitzrayim

Dam: The blood of devastating wars, choking the lifesprings that could nurture the world;

Tze-far-de-a: The frogs of fertility uncontrolled, animal passions on the rampage in a lusting world;

Ki-nim: Dust of the land cultivated too heavily or not enough, poisoned by pesticides which sicken those who labor in the field and those who eat its fruit;

A-rov: Swarms of ill and homeless people, reduced to foraging like animals, starving in a world of plenty;

De-ver: Pestilence of additives in all our food, unnaturally fattening cows, unhealthily fattening us;

She-chin: Soot and chemicals from factories and cars vomited into the sky, returning to attack our lungs, our skin, our bones;

Ba-rad: Hail from acid rain, harbingers of missiles that will send firestorms against our cities;

Cho-shech: Dark hatred of nations, peoples, lifestyles, sexual practices, or disabilities different from our own;

Ma-kat Be-cho-rot: First-born babies swollen from malnutrition, dead in sobbing mothers' arms. . . .

DAYENU (It Would Have Been Enough for Us)

In contrast to the plagues sent against the Egyptians—

כַּמָּה מַעֲלוֹת טוֹבוֹת לַמָּקוֹם עָלֵינוּ:

How many advantages did the Omnipresent shower upon us!

אִלּוּ הוֹצִיאָנוּ מִמִּצְרַיִם וְלֹא עָשָׂה בָהֶם שְׁפָטִים דַּיֵּנוּ:

I-lu ho-tzi-a-nu mi-Mitz-ra-yim, ve-lo a-sa va-hem she-fa-tim, Da-ye-nu!

If You had brought us out of Mitzrayim but had not executed judgment upon its people, *Dayenu!*

אִלּוּ עָשָׂה בָהֶם שְׁפָטִים וְלֹא עָשָׂה בֵאלֹהֵיהֶם דַּיֵּנוּ:

I-lu a-sa va-hem she-fa-tim, ve-lo a-sa vei-lo-hei-hem,
Da-yenu!

If you had executed judgment upon its people but not upon
their gods, *Dayenu!*

אִלּוּ עָשָׂה בֵאלֹהֵיהֶם וְלֹא הָרַג אֶת־בְּכוֹרֵיהֶם דַּיֵּנוּ:

I-lu a-sa vei-lo-hei-hem, ve-lo ha-rag et be-cho-rei-hem,
Da-ye-nu!

If You had executed judgment upon their gods, but had not
executed their first-born, *Dayenu!*

אִלּוּ הָרַג אֶת בְּכוֹרֵיהֶם וְלֹא נָתַן לָנוּ אֶת־מָמוֹנָם דַּיֵּנוּ:

I-lu ha-rag et be-cho-rei-hem, ve-lo na-tan la-nu et ma-
mo-nam, Da-ye-nu!

If You had executed their first-born, but had not given us
their possessions, *Dayenu!*

אִלּוּ נָתַן לָנוּ אֶת־מָמוֹנָם וְלֹא קָרַע לָנוּ אֶת־הַיָּם דַּיֵּנוּ:

I-lu na-tan la-nu et ma-mo-nam, ve-lo ka-ra la-nu et ha-
yam, Da-ye-nu!

If You had given us their possessions, but had not split the
Sea for us, *Dayenu!*

אִלּוּ קָרַע לָנוּ אֶת־הַיָּם וְלֹא הֶעֱבִירָנוּ בְתוֹכוֹ בֶּחָרָבָה
דַּיֵּנוּ:

I-lu ka-ra la-nu et ha-yam, ve-lo he-e-vi-ra-nu ve-to-cha
ve-cha-ra-va, Da-ye-nu!

If You had split the Sea for us, but had not let us pass
through its depths on dry land, *Dayenu!*

אִלּוּ הֶעֱבִירָנוּ בְתוֹכוֹ בֶּחָרָבָה וְלֹא שִׁקַּע צָרֵינוּ בְּתוֹכוֹ
דַּיֵּנוּ:

I-lu he-e-vi-ra-nu ve-to-cho ve-cha-ra-va, ve-lo shi-ka
tza-rei-nu be-to-cha, Da-ye-nu!

If You had let us pass through its depths on dry land, but
had not drowned our oppressors in its depths, *Dayenu!*

אִלּוּ שִׁקַּע צָרֵינוּ בְתוֹכוֹ וְלֹא סִפֵּק צָרְכֵּנוּ בַּמִּדְבָּר
אַרְבָּעִים שָׁנָה דַּיֵּנוּ:

I-lu shi-ka tza-rei-nu be-to-cho, ve-lo si-pek tzor-kei-nu
ba-mid-bar ar-ba-im sha-na, Da-ye-nu!

If You had drowned our oppressors in its depths, but had not
provided for our needs in the wilderness for forty years,
Dayenu!

אִלּוּ סִפֵּק צָרְכֵּנוּ בַּמִּדְבָּר אַרְבָּעִים שָׁנָה וְלֹא הֶאֱכִילָנוּ
אֶת־הַמָּן דַּיֵּנוּ:

I-lu si-pek tzor-kei-nu ba-mid-bar ar-ba-im sha-na, ve-lo
he-e-chi-la-nu et ha-man, Da-ye-nu!

If You had provided for our needs in the wilderness for forty
years, but had not fed us manna, *Dayenu!*

אִלּוּ הֶאֱכִילָנוּ אֶת־הַמָּן וְלֹא נָתַן לָנוּ אֶת־הַשַּׁבָּת דַּיֵּנוּ:

I-lu he-e-chi-la-nu et ha-man, ve-lo na-tan la-nu et ha-
Sha-bat, Da-ye-nu!

If You had fed us manna, but had not given us Shabbat,
Dayenu!

אִלּוּ נָתַן לָנוּ אֶת־הַשַּׁבָּת וְלֹא קֵרְבָנוּ לִפְנֵי הַר סִינַי דַּיֵּנוּ:

I-lu na-tan la-nu et ha-Sha-bat, ve-lo kei-re-va-nu lif-nei
Har Si-nai, Da-ye-nu!

If You had given us Shabbat, but had not drawn us near the
face of Mount Sinai, *Dayenu!*

אִלּוּ קֵרְבָנוּ לִפְנֵי הַר סִינַי וְלֹא נָתַן לָנוּ אֶת־הַתּוֹרָה דַּיֵּנוּ:

I-lu kei-re-va-nu lif-nei Har Si-nai, ve-lo na-tan la-nu et ha-To-rah, Da-ye-nu!

If You had drawn us near the face of Mount Sinai, but had not given us the Torah, *Dayenu!*

אִלּוּ נָתַן לָנוּ אֶת־הַתּוֹרָה וְלֹא הִכְנִיסָנוּ לְאֶרֶץ יִשְׂרָאֵל דַּיֵּנוּ:

I-lu na-tan la-nu et ha-To-rah, ve-lo hich-ni-sa-nu le-E-retz Yis-ra-el, Da-ye-nu!

If You had given us the Torah, but had not brought us into the Land of Israel, *Dayenu!*

אִלּוּ הִכְנִיסָנוּ לְאֶרֶץ יִשְׂרָאֵל וְלֹא בָנָה לָנוּ אֶת־בֵּית הַבְּחִירָה דַּיֵּנוּ:

I-lu hich-ni-sa-nu le-E-retz Yis-ra-el, ve-lo va-nah la-nu et Bet Ha-be-chi-ra, Da-ye-nu!

If You had brought us into the Land of Israel, but had not built for us Your chosen House, the Temple, *Dayenu!*

עַל־אַחַת כַּמָּה וְכַמָּה טוֹבָה כְפוּלָה וּמְכֻפֶּלֶת לַמָּקוֹם עָלֵינוּ. שֶׁהוֹצִיאָנוּ מִמִּצְרַיִם. וְעָשָׂה בָהֶם שְׁפָטִים. וְעָשָׂה בֵאלֹהֵיהֶם. וְהָרַג אֶת־בְּכוֹרֵיהֶם. וְנָתַן לָנוּ אֶת־מָמוֹנָם. וְקָרַע לָנוּ אֶת־הַיָּם. וְהֶעֱבִירָנוּ בְתוֹכוֹ בֶחָרָבָה. וְשִׁקַּע צָרֵינוּ בְּתוֹכוֹ. וְסִפֵּק צָרְכֵּנוּ בַּמִּדְבָּר אַרְבָּעִים שָׁנָה. וְהֶאֱכִילָנוּ אֶת־הַמָּן. וְנָתַן לָנוּ אֶת־הַשַּׁבָּת. וְקֵרְבָנוּ לִפְנֵי הַר סִינַי. וְנָתַן לָנוּ אֶת־הַתּוֹרָה. וְהִכְנִיסָנוּ לְאֶרֶץ יִשְׂרָאֵל. וּבָנָה לָנוּ אֶת־בֵּית הַבְּחִירָה. לְכַפֵּר עַל־כָּל־עֲוֹנוֹתֵינוּ:

How much greater, many times greater, is the good which the Omnipresent showered upon us, for God *did* each one of these favors for us, and many more:

You *did* bring us out of Mitzrayim, execute judgments upon its people, their gods, and their first-born;

You *did* give us their possessions, split the Sea, let us pass through its depths on dry land, and drowned our oppressors in its depths;

You *did* provide for our needs in the wilderness for forty years, feed us manna, and give us Shabbat;

You *did* draw us near the face of Mount Sinai, give us the Torah, bring us into the Land of Israel, and build for us Your chosen House, the Temple

To atone for all our wrongs.

*   *   *   *   *

RABBAN GAMLIEL'S INSTRUCTIONS

Reflections

But we must not let the story separate us from the meal. Rabban Gamliel (Mishna Pesachim 10:5) returns us to the foods before us, the relics of the first Seder, storehouses of memory from our suffering and our redemption. So crucial is the tie between the foods and the story that:

רַבָּן גַּמְלִיאֵל הָיָה אוֹמֵר: כָּל־שֶׁלֹּא אָמַר שְׁלֹשָׁה דְבָרִים
אֵלּוּ בַּפֶּסַח לֹא יָצָא יְדֵי חוֹבָתוֹ: וְאֵלּוּ הֵן.

פֶּסַח.   מַצָּה.   וּמָרוֹר:

Rabban Gamliel used to say that all those who had not spoken of three words on Pesach had not fulfilled their obligation to tell the story. These are:

Pesach   Matzah   Maror

Pesach

DIRECTIONS: All present direct their attention to the shankbone, but do not touch
or raise it.

פֶּסַח שֶׁהָיוּ אֲבוֹתֵינוּ (וְאִמּוֹתֵינוּ) אוֹכְלִים בִּזְמַן שֶׁבֵּית
הַמִּקְדָּשׁ הָיָה קַיָּם עַל־שׁוּם מָה. עַל־שׁוּם שֶׁפָּסַח הַקָּדוֹשׁ
בָּרוּךְ הוּא עַל־בָּתֵּי אֲבוֹתֵינוּ (וְאִמּוֹתֵינוּ) בְּמִצְרָיִם.
שֶׁנֶּאֱמַר: וַאֲמַרְתֶּם זֶבַח־פֶּסַח הוּא לַיְיָ אֲשֶׁר פָּסַח
עַל־בָּתֵּי בְנֵי־יִשְׂרָאֵל בְּמִצְרַיִם בְּנָגְפּוֹ אֶת־מִצְרַיִם וְאֶת־
בָּתֵּינוּ הִצִּיל. וַיִּקֹּד הָעָם וַיִּשְׁתַּחֲווּ:

The Pesach which our ancestors ate while the Temple stood:
for what reason is it?

For the reason that the Blessed Holy One passed over (*pa-
sach*) the houses of our ancestors in Mitzrayim, as it is said:
"And you shall say, 'It is the Passover offering for Adonai,
who passed over the houses of the Israelites in Mitzrayim
and smote the Egyptians but saved our houses.' And the
people bowed their heads and bent their knees in prayer."
(Exodus 12:27)

Reflections

While the Matzah and the Maror, which are still eaten today, will soon
be raised and shown to the Seder participants, the Shankbone (*ze-ro-a*)
remains on the Seder plate, the still bone of an offering that was once a
vigorous limb of our life with God. One day, as in the Valley of Ezekiel's
vision, this dry bone too will live again, clothed in the flesh of whatever
offerings God desires for the future. Till that time of awakening it will
sleep, and we leave it in its place, undisturbed.

Matzah

DIRECTIONS: The plate of matzah is raised.

מַצָּה זוֹ שֶׁאָנוּ אוֹכְלִים עַל־שׁוּם מָה. עַל־שׁוּם שֶׁלֹּא
הִסְפִּיק בְּצֵקָם שֶׁל־אֲבוֹתֵינוּ (וְאִמּוֹתֵינוּ) לְהַחֲמִיץ עַד־
שֶׁנִּגְלָה עֲלֵיהֶם מֶלֶךְ מַלְכֵי הַמְּלָכִים הַקָּדוֹשׁ בָּרוּךְ הוּא

וּגְאָלָם. שֶׁנֶּאֱמַר: וַיֹּאפוּ אֶת־הַבָּצֵק אֲשֶׁר הוֹצִיאוּ
מִמִּצְרַיִם עֻגֹת מַצּוֹת כִּי לֹא חָמֵץ. כִּי־גֹרְשׁוּ מִמִּצְרַיִם
וְלֹא יָכְלוּ לְהִתְמַהְמֵהַּ וְגַם־צֵדָה לֹא־עָשׂוּ לָהֶם:

This Matzah, this unleavened bread, that we eat, for what reason is it?

For the reason that there was not sufficient time for the dough of our ancestors to leaven when the Sovereign of all earthly sovereigns, the Blessed Holy One, was revealed to us and redeemed us, as it is said: "And they baked the dough which they brought forth out of Mitzrayim into matzah cakes (cakes of unleavened bread) which had not fermented, for having been driven out of Mitzrayim they could not tarry, and no provisions had they made for themselves." (Exodus 12:39)

Maror

DIRECTIONS: The maror is raised.

מָרוֹר זֶה שֶׁאָנוּ אוֹכְלִים עַל־שׁוּם מָה. עַל־שׁוּם שֶׁמֵּרְרוּ
הַמִּצְרִים אֶת־חַיֵּי אֲבוֹתֵינוּ (וְאִמּוֹתֵינוּ) בְּמִצְרָיִם.
שֶׁנֶּאֱמַר: וַיְמָרְרוּ אֶת־חַיֵּיהֶם בַּעֲבוֹדָה קָשָׁה בְּחֹמֶר
וּבִלְבֵנִים וּבְכָל־עֲבֹדָה בַּשָּׂדֶה. אֵת כָּל־עֲבֹדָתָם אֲשֶׁר־
עָבְדוּ בָהֶם בְּפָרֶךְ:

This Maror, this bitter vegetable, that we eat, for what reason is it?

For the reason that the Egyptians embittered (*mei-re-ru*, the root of *maror*) the lives of our ancestors in Mitzrayim, as it is said: "And they embittered their lives with servitude hardened in mortar and bricks, with every servitude in the field, with torment." (Exodus 1:14)

(By raising up these foods, eaten so long ago and remaining on our Seder table to this very night, we connect ourselves to the anguish and the ecstasy of those who first raised them up, who first transformed ordinary flatbread and an ordinary vegetable into experiences of God's power to transform poverty and bitterness into freedom and courage. For:)

בְּכָל־דּוֹר וָדוֹר חַיָּב אָדָם לִרְאוֹת אֶת־עַצְמוֹ כְּאִלּוּ הוּא יָצָא מִמִּצְרָיִם.

Be-chol dor va-dor cha-yav a-dam lir-ot et atz-mo ke-i-lu hu ya-tza mi-Mitz-ra-yim.

In every single generation every single one of us is obligated to view ourselves as though we had gone forth from Mitzrayim.

שֶׁנֶּאֱמַר: וְהִגַּדְתָּ לְבִנְךָ בַּיּוֹם הַהוּא לֵאמֹר. בַּעֲבוּר זֶה עָשָׂה יְיָ לִי בְּצֵאתִי מִמִּצְרָיִם:

As it is said: "And you shall tell your child in that day, saying these words: "Because of this which Adonai did for *me* in bringing me out of Mitzrayim." (Exodus 13:8)

לֹא אֶת־אֲבוֹתֵינוּ (וְאֶת־אִמּוֹתֵינוּ) בִּלְבַד גָּאַל הַקָּדוֹשׁ בָּרוּךְ הוּא. אֶלָּא אַף אוֹתָנוּ גָּאַל עִמָּהֶם. שֶׁנֶּאֱמַר: וְאוֹתָנוּ הוֹצִיא מִשָּׁם. לְמַעַן הָבִיא אוֹתָנוּ לָתֵת לָנוּ אֶת־הָאָרֶץ אֲשֶׁר נִשְׁבַּע לַאֲבֹתֵינוּ (וּלְאִמּוֹתֵינוּ):

Not our ancestors alone did the Blessed Holy One redeem, but us too did God redeem along with them, as it is said: "And God brought *us* out of there, in order to bring *us* in, to give *us* the land sworn to our ancestors." (Deuteronomy 6:23)

Reflections

And so the divisions of the Four Children have been overcome: beyond the four different answers to the four different children lies this single answer now revealed, from Deuteronomy 6:23: "God brought *us* out of there, in order to bring *us* in." By telling the story together, wise and wicked, simple and unable to speak, we have *all* acquired the merit to be redeemed. The Magid, the story of the Exodus, reunites the Jewish people.

Culmination of the Story: Psalms of Praise

Reflections

We have reached the joyous climax of the Magid: the recognition that, as a result of our redemption from the physical and spiritual constrictions of Mitzrayim, we have broken through into the broad place of the realm of God, where the most natural thing in the world is to sing praise to our Redeemer.

*   *   *   *   *

When we began the story we raised the cup and covered the matzot, the bread of affliction; now once more, in the presence of the lifted cup, we cover the matzot, for their tale is complete: they have been transformed into the bread of freedom. The raised cup reminds us of the eternal presence of the holy God, now in freedom as earlier in affliction.

DIRECTIONS: The plate of matzah is covered as all raise their cups of wine.

לְפִיכָךְ אֲנַחְנוּ חַיָּבִים לְהוֹדוֹת, לְהַלֵּל לְשַׁבֵּחַ, לְפָאֵר,
לְרוֹמֵם, לְהַדֵּר, לְבָרֵךְ, לְעַלֵּה, וּלְקַלֵּס, לְמִי שֶׁעָשָׂה
לַאֲבוֹתֵינוּ (וּלְאִמּוֹתֵינוּ) וְלָנוּ אֶת־כָּל־הַנִּסִּים הָאֵלֶּה.
הוֹצִיאָנוּ מֵעַבְדוּת לְחֵרוּת. מִיָּגוֹן לְשִׂמְחָה. מֵאֵבֶל לְיוֹם
טוֹב. וּמֵאֲפֵלָה לְאוֹר גָּדוֹל. וּמִשִּׁעְבּוּד לִגְאֻלָּה. וְנֹאמַר
לְפָנָיו שִׁירָה חֲדָשָׁה הַלְלוּיָהּ:

Therefore we are obligated to thank, sing hallel, praise, glorify, exalt, honor, bless, elevate, and shout for joy to the One who made all these miracles for our ancestors and for us! You brought us
>from human servitude to freedom
>from sorrow to joy
>from a time of mourning to a festive day
>from deep darkness to great light
>and from slavery to redemption!
And so in Your presence we renew our song:
>Hallelu-Ya! Sing Hallel to Ya!

Song: Ve-no-mar le-fa-nav shi-ra cha-da-sha, Ha-le-lu-Ya.
(In Your presence we renew our song: Halleluya, Praise God!)

Psalm 113

הַלְלוּיָהּ

הַלְלוּ עַבְדֵי יְיָ. הַלְלוּ אֶת־שֵׁם יְיָ:

יְהִי שֵׁם יְיָ מְבֹרָךְ מֵעַתָּה וְעַד עוֹלָם:

מִמִּזְרַח־שֶׁמֶשׁ עַד־מְבוֹאוֹ מְהֻלָּל שֵׁם יְיָ:

רָם עַל־כָּל־גּוֹיִם יְיָ עַל־הַשָּׁמַיִם כְּבוֹדוֹ:

מִי כַּיְיָ אֱלֹהֵינוּ הַמַּגְבִּיהִי לָשָׁבֶת:

הַמַּשְׁפִּילִי לִרְאוֹת בַּשָּׁמַיִם וּבָאָרֶץ:

מְקִימִי מֵעָפָר דָּל מֵאַשְׁפֹּת יָרִים אֶבְיוֹן:

לְהוֹשִׁיבִי עִם־נְדִיבִים עִם נְדִיבֵי עַמּוֹ:

מוֹשִׁיבִי עֲקֶרֶת הַבַּיִת אֵם־הַבָּנִים שְׂמֵחָה הַלְלוּיָהּ:

Halleluya!

Sing Hallel, those who serve not Pharaoh but Adonai,
Sing Hallel to the Eternal Name,
May it be praised in all its power
From now until eternity, in this place and every place,
From the sea where the sun rises to the sea where it sets,
In all the lands between
Is Hallel sung to Adonai!

Greater than all the nations are You, Adonai,
Your glory is higher than the heavens;
Who is like You, Eternal One, our caring, compassionate
    God?
You dwell in the highest places,
You are present in the humblest places, surveying heaven
    from the earth, the earth from heaven!
You gently lift the poor from the dust,
From the ash heap You display the divinity of the needy,
Seating them with nobility, with the most noble of Your
    people,
Inviting every barren woman in Your house
To take her place as a mother overjoyed
At all the children she has the power to nurture,
Halleluya!

Psalm 114

בְּצֵאת יִשְׂרָאֵל מִמִּצְרָיִם בֵּית יַעֲקֹב מֵעַם לֹעֵז:
הָיְתָה יְהוּדָה לְקָדְשׁוֹ יִשְׂרָאֵל מַמְשְׁלוֹתָיו:
הַיָּם רָאָה וַיָּנֹס הַיַּרְדֵּן יִסֹּב לְאָחוֹר:
הֶהָרִים רָקְדוּ כְאֵילִים גְּבָעוֹת כִּבְנֵי־צֹאן:
מַה־לְּךָ הַיָּם כִּי תָנוּס הַיַּרְדֵּן תִּסֹּב לְאָחוֹר:
הֶהָרִים תִּרְקְדוּ כְאֵילִים גְּבָעוֹת כִּבְנֵי־צֹאן:
מִלִּפְנֵי אָדוֹן חוּלִי אָרֶץ מִלִּפְנֵי אֱלוֹהַּ יַעֲקֹב:
הַהֹפְכִי הַצּוּר אֲגַם־מָיִם חַלָּמִישׁ לְמַעְיְנוֹ מָיִם:

Be-tzeit Yis-ra-el mi-Mitz-ra-yim
Beit Ya-a-kov me-am lo-ez.
Ha-ye-ta Ye-hu-da le-kod-sho
Yis-ra-el mam-she-lo-tav,
Ha-yam ra-a va-ya-nos
Ha-Yar-den yi-sov le-a-chor. (Be-tzeit Yis-ra-el . . .)

He-ha-rim ra-ke-du che-ei-lim,
Ge-va-ot ki-ve-nei tzon.
Ma le-cha ha-yam ki ta-nus,
Ha-Yar-den ti-sov le-a-chor. (Be-tzeit Yis-ra-el . . .)

He-ha-rim tir-ke-du che-ei-lim,
Ge-va-ot ki-ve-nei tzon,
Mi-lif-nei a-don chu-li a-retz
Mi-lif-nei E-lo-ha Ya-a-kov. (Be-tzeit Yis-ra-el . . .)

Ha-hof-chi ha-tzur a-gam ma-yim
Cha-la-mish le-ma-ye-no ma-yim. (Be-tzeit Yis-ra-el . . .)

When Israel went forth from Mitzrayim,
The House of Jacob from a people speaking a strange
    tongue,
Judah became the place from which God's holiness went
    forth,
Israel the seat
From which the nations knew God's rule.

The sea looked—
And fled!

The Jordan is turning back!
The mountains danced like rams,
The hills like lambs!
What is happening to you, O sea, that you are fleeing,
O Jordan, that you are turning back?
Mountains, that you are dancing like rams,
Hills, like lambs?

Before the face of Your Creator
Whirl about, O earth,
Before the face of the God of Jacob
Turning rocks to swirling pools of water,
Flinty stone to a flowing spring!

THE SECOND CUP: Deliverance

(The cup that was poured as we began the Magid, when the Four Questions were asked, is now to be drunk as we conclude the Magid. This
cup has witnessed the tale of God's deliverance of our people from the
Egyptian Mitzrayim; it offers hope that we may be delivered from all the
afflictions that delay the ultimate redemption, that keep the holy city
divided, and prevent the realization of the House of Ultimate Worship.)

DIRECTIONS: Before drinking the Second Cup, *Ve-hi-tzal-ti*, "I will deliver you
from their service" (Exodus 6:6), raise your cups and celebrate with the following words:

בָּרוּךְ אַתָּה יְיָ אֱלֹהֵינוּ מֶלֶךְ הָעוֹלָם. אֲשֶׁר גְּאָלָנוּ וְגָאַל
אֶת־אֲבוֹתֵינוּ (וְאֶת־אִמּוֹתֵנוּ) מִמִּצְרַיִם וְהִגִּיעָנוּ הַלַּיְלָה
הַזֶּה לֶאֱכָל־בּוֹ מַצָּה וּמָרוֹר. כֵּן יְיָ אֱלֹהֵינוּ וֵאלֹהֵי
אֲבוֹתֵינוּ (וְאִמּוֹתֵינוּ) יַגִּיעֵנוּ לְמוֹעֲדִים וְלִרְגָלִים אֲחֵרִים
הַבָּאִים לִקְרָאתֵנוּ לְשָׁלוֹם שְׂמֵחִים בְּבִנְיַן עִירֶךְ וְשָׂשִׂים
בַּעֲבוֹדָתֶךָ. וְנֹאכַל שָׁם מִן הַזְּבָחִים וּמִן הַפְּסָחִים אֲשֶׁר
יַגִּיעַ דָּמָם עַל־קִיר מִזְבַּחֲךָ לְרָצוֹן. וְנוֹדֶה לְךָ שִׁיר חָדָשׁ
עַל־גְּאֻלָּתֵנוּ וְעַל פְּדוּת נַפְשֵׁנוּ: בָּרוּךְ אַתָּה יְיָ גָּאַל
יִשְׂרָאֵל:

Ba-ruch a-ta A-do-nai E-lo-hei-nu me-lech ha-o-lam, a-sher ge-a-la-nu ve-ga-al et a-vo-tei-nu (ve-et i-mo-tei-nu) mi-Mitz-ra-yim, ve-hi-gi-a-nu ha-lai-la ha-zeh le-e-chol bo ma-tzah u-ma-ror. Ken A-do-nai E-lo-hei-nu ve-lo-hei a-vo-tei-nu (ve-i-mo-tei-nu) ya-gi-ei-nu le-mo-a-dim ve-li-re-ga-lim a-chei-rim ha-ba-im lik-ra-tei-nu le-sha-lom, se-mei-chim be-vin-yan i-re-cha, ve-sa-sim ba-a-vo-da-te-cha, ve-no-chal sham min ha-ze-va-chim u-min ha-pe-sa-chim a-sher ya-gi-a da-mam al kir miz-ba-cha-cha le-ra-tzon, ve-no-deh le-cha shir cha-dash al ge-u-la-tei-nu ve-al pe-dut naf-shei-nu. Ba-ruch a-ta A-do-nai, ga-al Yis-ra-el.

You are praised, Adonai our God, ruler over space and time,
Who has redeemed us in redeeming our fathers and mothers
From Mitzrayim,
And has brought us tonight
To the moment of eating matzah and maror.

Just so, Adonai our God and God of our mothers and
    fathers,
May You bring us to other seasons and festivals,
May they come to us in a time of peace,
Finding us joyful in building Your city,
Jubilant in serving You alone.

And may we be able to eat from all the offerings You desire at
    this season,
Brought before You in just the manner You command.
May we offer You, in thanks, our song renewed
For the redemption of our bodies and our souls.

בָּרוּךְ אַתָּה יְיָ אֱלֹהֵינוּ מֶלֶךְ הָעוֹלָם. בּוֹרֵא פְּרִי הַגָּפֶן:

Ba-ruch a-ta A-do-nai E-lo-hei-nu me-lech ha-o-lam, bo-rei pe-ri ha-ga-fen.

Praised are You, Adonai our God, Monarch over time and space, Creator of this fruit of the vine.

DIRECTIONS: Drink from the Second Cup, *Ve-hi-tzal-ti*, "I will deliver you from their service," while reclining to the left, tasting the holy joy of our deliverance from affliction.

רְחָצָה

RA-CHA-TZA

Dip Hands
(Washing Before the Meal)

Introduction by the Song

הִנָּךְ יָפָה רַעְיָתִי הִנָּךְ יָפָה עֵינַיִךְ יוֹנִים מִבַּעַד לְצַמָּתֵךְ
שַׂעְרֵךְ כְּעֵדֶר הָעִזִּים שֶׁגָּלְשׁוּ מֵהַר גִּלְעָד: שִׁנַּיִךְ כְּעֵדֶר
הַקְּצוּבוֹת שֶׁעָלוּ מִן־הָרַחְצָה:

How splendid you are, my beloved,
How splendid you are!
From behind your cloak your eyes are doves,
Your hair descends upon your shoulders
Like a flood of goats cascading down the crags,
Your white teeth are like shorn ewes
Glistening
As they come up out of the washing!
(Song of Songs 4:1-2)

* * * * *

Reflections

And so God has brought us to the moment of eating matzah. We
have looked at it, raised it on the plate, smelled its fragrance,
heard its crumbling as we broke off the afikomon—but like slaves
at the master's table we could neither touch nor taste.

This table from which we eat, like every Jewish dining table, par-
takes of the table of offerings in the Temple. Before eating, the
kohanim, the priests, would pour the waters of life over their
hands, and without a word—that the pouring might connect intimately with the eating—they would silently take hold of their
piece of freedom and break the stillness only with the praise of
God we know as "Motzi." This blessing anticipates the time when
God will recreate the freedom of Eden, when without the sweat of
human toil bread itself will spring up directly from the earth. Let

us now wash as they did, listening in silence to the delicious expectation of freedom before we praise the One who made us free.

DIRECTIONS: Using a cup or pitcher, the leader should pour fresh water over each hand, either on behalf of the Seder participants, or in company with them. As in Urechatz, participants may also be encouraged to pour the water over the hands of their neighbors. As the washers raise their hands to dry them, say the following:

בָּרוּךְ אַתָּה יְיָ אֱלֹהֵינוּ מֶלֶךְ הָעוֹלָם. אֲשֶׁר קִדְּשָׁנוּ בְּמִצְוֹתָיו וְצִוָּנוּ עַל נְטִילַת יָדָיִם:

Ba-ruch a-ta A-do-nai E-lo-hei-nu me-lech ha-o-lam, a-sher ki-de-sha-nu be-mitz-vo-tav ve-tzi-va-nu al ne-ti-lat ya-da-yim.

You are praised, Adonai our God, Monarch of time and space, who shares Your holiness with us through Your mitzvot, and now bestows on us the mitzvah of washing our hands.

DIRECTIONS: All remain silent till the moment of saying Motzi.

מוֹצִיא

MO-TZI

Praise God for Bread

DIRECTIONS: The leader holds the top and bottom matzah, the unbroken matzahs representing freedom, and all say together:

בָּרוּךְ אַתָּה יְיָ אֱלֹהֵינוּ מֶלֶךְ הָעוֹלָם. הַמּוֹצִיא לֶחֶם מִן הָאָרֶץ:

Ba-ruch a-ta A-do-nai E-lo-hei-nu me-lech ha-o-lam, ha-mo-tzi le-chem min ha-a-retz.

You are praised, Adonai our God, Monarch of time and space, who is bringing forth bread from the earth.

מַצָּה

MA-TZAH

With Freedom's Matzah We Are Fed

DIRECTIONS: The leader now replaces the bottom matzah with the middle, broken, one, representing slavery, and all say together:

בָּרוּךְ אַתָּה יְיָ אֱלֹהֵינוּ מֶלֶךְ הָעוֹלָם. אֲשֶׁר קִדְּשָׁנוּ
בְּמִצְוֹתָיו וְצִוָּנוּ עַל אֲכִילַת מַצָּה:

Ba-ruch a-ta A-do-nai E-lo-hei-nu me-lech ha-o-lam, a-sher ki-de-sha-nu be-mitz-vo-tav ve-tzi-va-nu al a-chi-lat ma-tzah.

You are praised, Adonai our God, Monarch of time and space, who shares Your holiness with us through Your mitzvot, and now bestows on us the mitzvah of eating matzah.

DIRECTIONS: The leader distributes olive-sized pieces of the top matzah (freedom) and the middle matzah (slavery) to each participant. Reclining to the left, all eat the two pieces of matzah, our teeth transforming slavery into freedom.

מָרוֹר

MA-ROR

To eat the bitter herb we strain
That we might taste brickmakers' pain

(Bitter Herb and Charoset)

Introduction by the Song

מְצָאֻנִי הַשֹּׁמְרִים הַסֹּבְבִים בָּעִיר הִכּוּנִי פְצָעוּנִי נָשְׂאוּ
אֶת־רְדִידִי מֵעָלַי שֹׁמְרֵי הַחֹמוֹת: הִשְׁבַּעְתִּי אֶתְכֶם בְּנוֹת
יְרוּשָׁלָיִם אִם־תִּמְצְאוּ אֶת־דּוֹדִי מַה־תַּגִּידוּ לוֹ שֶׁחוֹלַת

אֲהֵבָה אָנִי: סָמְכוּנִי בָּאֲשִׁישׁוֹת רַפְּדוּנִי בַּתַּפּוּחִים כִּי־
חוֹלַת אַהֲבָה אָנִי:

The guards have found me,
They surround me in the city,
They hit me, bruised me,
Tore off my clothes—
O, these guards of the walls!
Give me your oath, O daughters of Jerusalem,
That you will find my beloved!
What tale should you tell?
That I am sick with love!
Sustain me with raisins,
Nourish me with apples,
For I am sick with love.

(Song of Songs 5:7-8; 2:5)

Reflections on the Bitter . . .

Having said Motzi, we continue with our meal. But a strange appetizer awaits us: *maror*, the bitter vegetable, a sharp reminder that the matzah of freedom often needs roots of bitterness from which to sprout.

Many of us here have personally known the bitterness of pain, of disappointment, of loss. If we have been fortunate, we have learned from our pain, matured through our disappointment, compensated for our loss through a new awareness of our own strength. Bitterness, we have learned, can be transformed into a blessing—and that is why we offer a blessing when we eat the bitter herb.

Thank You, Sovereign of all existence, for the understanding and compassion that can be released when we eat the fruit of bitterness.

. . . And the Sweet

The charoset,
A mixture of apples, nuts, wine, and spices,
Represents the mixture of clay and straw
From which in bondage
We made our bricks.
It recalls as well
The women of Israel
Who bore their children secretly
Beneath the apple trees of Mitzrayim.

And like the apple tree,
Which brings forth fruit and only then
Sprouts leaves to protect it,
Our heroic mothers bore children
Without any assurance of security or safety.
We recall this beautiful, militant devotion
Which sweetened the misery of slavery
As we dip our bitters
In the sweet charoset.
It is the story of this night:
Bitter and sweet,
Sadness and joy,
Tales of shame that end
In praise.

It is the story of our life.

*   *   *   *   *

DIRECTIONS: Fresh horseradish or the hard core of romaine lettuce is taken and dipped into the charoset. Most of the charoset should be shaken off so that the bitter taste is not obliterated. Then say the following:

בָּרוּךְ אַתָּה יְיָ אֱלֹהֵינוּ מֶלֶךְ הָעוֹלָם. אֲשֶׁר קִדְּשָׁנוּ
בְּמִצְוֹתָיו וְצִוָּנוּ עַל אֲכִילַת מָרוֹר:

Ba-ruch a-ta A-do-nai E-lo-hei-nu me-lech ha-o-lam, a-sher ki-de-sha-nu be-mitz-vo-tav ve-tzi-va-nu al a-chi-lat ma-ror.

Praised are You, Adonai our God, ruler over time and space, who shares Your holiness with us through Your mitzvot, and now bestows on us the mitzvah of eating the bitter vegetable.

DIRECTIONS: Eat the maror brushed with charoset, but not in the reclining position of freedom.

כּוֹרֵךְ
KO-RECH

Hillel said: Mix herbs again
With matzah's promise: pain will end

Reflections

A remnant of the Temple lies before us on the plate. The Torah tells us
that the Pesach offering should be eaten *al* (literally, "over") matzah and
bitters. What does this mean? How exactly did God wish this crucial
offering to be eaten?

Some people ate one after the other, but not Hillel, the patient sage of the
first century B.C.E. who believed that the whole Torah was a commentary
on the principle that none of us should do to others what is hurtful to
ourselves. Hillel believed *al* should be taken literally, "on top of,"
mingling in the same mouthful everything represented by the Pesach
offering, the matzah of affliction and freedom, and the maror. Mixing
them (*korech*) prevented any one taste from dominating another.

Once the Temple was destroyed, the Pesach offering was no longer
brought: to us its taste is silent. Did it tend toward the matzah, toward
freedom, reflecting the rabbis' view that in killing the lamb the Israelites
had killed an Egyptian god? Or did the taste tend toward the maror, the
bitter memories of slavery that disfigured their lives even after they ate
the lamb and left Mitzrayim? Hillel's practice of *korech* suggests that
part of the challenge of living is to taste freedom even in the midst of
oppression, and to be ever conscious of the oppression of others even
when we are free.

DIRECTIONS: Each person is given a small piece of the bottom matzah and places
some maror upon it, perhaps of a different variety than before (using the
romaine lettuce in the Chazeret section of the Seder plate). All say together:

זֵכֶר לְמִקְדָּשׁ כְּהִלֵּל:

כֵּן עָשָׂה הִלֵּל בִּזְמַן שֶׁבֵּית הַמִּקְדָּשׁ הָיָה קַיָּם. הָיָה כּוֹרֵךְ
פֶּסַח מַצָּה וּמָרוֹר וְאוֹכֵל בְּיַחַד. לְקַיֵּם מַה שֶּׁנֶּאֱמַר:
עַל־מַצּוֹת וּמְרוֹרִים יֹאכְלֻהוּ:

Ze-cher le-mik-dash ke-Hil-lel:
Ken a-sa Hil-lel biz-man she-bet ha-mik-dash ha-ya ka-
yam. Ha-ya ko-rech pe-sach ma-tzah u-ma-ror ve-o-chel
be-ya-chad, le-ka-yem ma she-ne-e-mar: "Al ma-tzot
u-me-ro-rim yoch-lu-hu."

A remnant of the Temple, the Seat of Holiness
according to the practice of Hillel:

This is what Hillel the Elder used to do in the time that the
Holy Temple still stood. He would mix the Pesach offering
with matzah and maror and eat them together, so as properly
to carry out the Torah's injunction: "On matzah and bitters
they shall eat it." (Numbers 9:11)

DIRECTIONS: Eat the matzah and maror while reclining to the left.

שֻׁלְחָן עוֹרֵךְ

SHUL-CHAN O-RECH

The Tale Continues as We Dine

Introduction by the Song

עוּרִי צָפוֹן וּבוֹאִי תֵימָן הָפִיחִי גַנִּי יִזְּלוּ בְשָׂמָיו יָבֹא דוֹדִי
לְגַנּוֹ וְיֹאכַל פְּרִי מְגָדָיו: בָּאתִי לְגַנִּי אֲחוֹתִי כַלָּה אָרִיתִי
מוֹרִי עִם־בְּשָׂמִי אָכַלְתִּי יַעְרִי עִם־דִּבְשִׁי שָׁתִיתִי יֵינִי עִם־
חֲלָבִי אִכְלוּ רֵעִים שְׁתוּ וְשִׁכְרוּ דוֹדִים:

Stir yourself, north wind,
Come, O south,
Breathe upon my garden that the spices may flow out;
Let my beloved come into his garden
And taste its choicest fruits!

I have come to my garden, my sister, my bride,
I have been gathering my fragrant spices,
Eating my dripping honeycomb,

Drinking my creamy wine—
Now eat, good friends,
Drink your fill, beloved guests!

(Song of Songs 4:16–5:1)

* * * * *

The Leader Says:

The first part of the Seder is complete,
The time has come to enjoy our food.
But those who have prepared the food,
Who have spent days and weeks cleaning, chopping, slicing,
Cannot relax till all is served, tasted, judged:
"Will our offering be accepted?"
"Will people like the food we've cooked?"

The Preparers of the Meal Say:

We who have worked to bring this meal to you
Want to tell you that your presence here means much to us,
For though God has bestowed upon us all
The mitzvah of celebrating Pesach,
Were it not for you, our guests,
We could not do God's will.

The Guests Say:

Were it not for you, *we* could not do God's will.
The food you've cooked will be wonderful this year
Because you made it,
Because you wanted us to know the taste of freedom.

Thank you for our feast.

* * * * *

The Kabbalists say:
When we chew our food
We release the holy sparks that hide within,
Permitting them to soar aloft to join once more
The single holy light from which they sprang.

* * * * *

A prevalent custom among Ashkenazi Jews, whose roots lie in Central or Eastern Europe, is to eat hardboiled eggs dipped in salt water at this point in the Seder meal. The shape of the eggs suggests the cyclical return of spring and new hope; their mode of cooking suggests that the destiny of the Jewish people is not to be consumed by the boiling pressures of our history, but to be strengthened by them, even nourished by them, and by our example to give hope and nourishment to others.

(As a reminder that the meal we are about to consume is neither the conclusion of the Seder nor the main reason for it, it is appropriate to continue discussing the questions raised by the Haggadah for which there was insufficient time during the reading. The Seder meal is not a time for idle chatter, and surely not for gossip—it is important to remember that the Hallel psalms before and after the meal are not interrupted by our eating; rather, eating and the good talk which accompanies it are also intended as occasions for glorifying God and God's creations.

צָפוּן

TZA-FUN

Who Will the Hidden Matzah Find?

Introduction by the Song

יוֹנָתִי בְּחַגְוֵי הַסֶּלַע בְּסֵתֶר הַמַּדְרֵגָה הַרְאִינִי אֶת־מַרְאַיִךְ
הַשְׁמִיעִנִי אֶת־קוֹלֵךְ כִּי־קוֹלֵךְ עָרֵב וּמַרְאֵיךְ נָאוֶה:

O my dove, hidden in the rock,
Secreted in the cliff,
Show me your countenance,
Let me hear your voice!
For your voice is sweet,
And your countenance is lovely.

(Song of Songs 2:14)

OPTIONAL DIRECTIONS

As the meal draws to its close, guests should be reminded to save room for the real dessert, a bite of the afikomon, hidden [*tzafun*] through the meal. The afikomon, the final food eaten at the Seder, should be consumed with gusto and before midnight, like the Pesach offering which it symbolizes.

As children go in search of the afikomon, they remind us of all our searches for the values, the hopes, the fulfillments that despite our freedom still remain hidden from us. The Haggadah before the meal brought us from the slavery of Mitzrayim to the redemption; when the children produce the afikomon from hiding they introduce the themes of the Haggadah after the meal: despite the incompleteness of our redemption today, the afikomon suddenly discovered in its wrap can inspire us to the faith that the fulfillment of much that we desire lies within our grasp.

They've found it! Indeed, they're holding it for ransom! Sometimes the leader has a gift prepared, sometimes the children will bargain with the leader to share with them some special skill or talent that will induce them to return the afikomon and permit the Seder to continue.

DIRECTIONS: When the afikomon has been found and returned to the leader, an olive-size piece is distributed to each person, and all consume the afikomon with enthusiasm.

BA-RECH

Thank God for All Our Food

Birkat Ha-Mazon: Blessings After the Meal

DIRECTIONS: The third cup of wine, the Cup of Redemption, is poured. It will be drunk at the conclusion of Birkat Ha-Mazon, the Praise of God Who Feeds the World, which follows a meal begun with a Motzi.

Reflections

Miraculously the small afikomon was sufficient to feed every guest here tonight. The Birkat Ha-Mazon symbolizes God's miraculous promise to feed everyone in the world. Just as we distributed the afikomon tonight, this prayer is a challenge to the human race to fulfill its destiny of distributing God's bounty to all. This prayer is a song of hope that one day, as part of the ultimate redemption, our efforts may help eliminate the scourge of poverty from the earth.

SHIR HA-MA-A-LOT: A Song for Transcendings

שִׁיר הַמַּעֲלוֹת בְּשׁוּב יְיָ אֶת־שִׁיבַת צִיּוֹן הָיִינוּ כְּחֹלְמִים.
אָז יִמָּלֵא שְׂחוֹק פִּינוּ וּלְשׁוֹנֵנוּ רִנָּה. אָז יֹאמְרוּ בַגּוֹיִם
הִגְדִּיל יְיָ לַעֲשׂוֹת עִם אֵלֶּה. הִגְדִּיל יְיָ לַעֲשׂוֹת עִמָּנוּ הָיִינוּ
שְׂמֵחִים. שׁוּבָה יְיָ אֶת־שְׁבִיתֵנוּ כַּאֲפִיקִים בַּנֶּגֶב. הַזֹּרְעִים
בְּדִמְעָה בְּרִנָּה יִקְצֹרוּ. הָלוֹךְ יֵלֵךְ וּבָכֹה נֹשֵׂא מֶשֶׁךְ הַזָּרַע
בֹּא יָבֹא בְרִנָּה נֹשֵׂא אֲלֻמֹּתָיו.

Shir ha-ma-a-lot: be-shuv A-do-nai et shi-vat Tzi-yon
ha-yi-nu ke-chol-mim. Az yi-ma-lei se-chok pi-nu u-le-
sho-ne-nu ri-na. Az yom-ru va-go-yim hig-dil A-do-nai
la-a-sot im ei-leh, hig-dil A-do-nai la-a-sot i-ma-nu,
ha-yi-nu se-mei-chim. Shu-va A-do-nai et she-vi-tei-nu
ka-a-fi-kim ba-Ne-gev. Ha-zor-im be-di-mah be-ri-na
yik-tzo-ru. Ha-loch ye-lech u-va-cho no-sei me-shech ha-
za-rah bo ya-vo ve-ri-na no-sei a-lu-mo-tav.

When Adonai carried the captives back to Zion
We thought we were in a dream.
Our mouth was filled with laughter then,
Our tongue with song,
Among the nations there was wonder then:
"How grandly has God dealt with these people!"
How grandly has God dealt with us!
We were so happy. . . .

Carry our captives back, O God,
In torrents turning desert streams to flood,
Then those who sow with weeping
Will reap with joy,
Those who trudge the row, watering with tears their trail of
    seed,
When they come back that way again,
Will march with song, erect,
Their arms uplifted, sheaves piled high!

ZIMUN: Invitation to Praise the Provider

Leader

רַבּוֹתַי (חֲבֵרַי וַחֲבֵרוֹתַי, *or*) נְבָרֵךְ:

Ra-bo-tai (*or*, Cha-vei-rai va-cha-vei-ro-tai) ne-va-rech.

Friends, let us praise God!

Participants

יְהִי שֵׁם יְיָ מְבֹרָךְ מֵעַתָּה וְעַד-עוֹלָם:

Ye-hi shem A-do-nai me-vo-rach me-a-ta ve-ad o-lam.

Let the Name of God be praised from this moment to the end of time.

Leader

בִּרְשׁוּת מָרָנָן וְרַבָּנָן וְרַבּוֹתַי (בִּרְשׁוּת חֲבֵרַי וַחֲבֵרוֹתַי, *or*)
נְבָרֵךְ (אֱלֹהֵינוּ, *if ten or more are present*) שֶׁאָכַלְנוּ מִשֶּׁלּוֹ:

Bir-shut ma-ra-nan ve-ra-ba-nan ve-ra-bo-tai (*or*, Bir-shut cha-vei-rai ve-cha-vei-ro-tai), ne-va-rech (*if ten or more are present*, E-lo-hei-nu) she-a-chal-nu mi-she-lo.

With the permission of our friends here gathered, let us praise (*if ten or more are present*, our God,) the One of whose bounty we have eaten.

Participants

בָּרוּךְ (אֱלֹהֵינוּ, *if ten or more are present*) שֶׁאָכַלְנוּ
מִשֶּׁלּוֹ וּבְטוּבוֹ חָיִינוּ:

Ba-ruch (*if ten or more are present*, E-lo-hei-nu) she-a-chal-nu mi-she-lo, u-ve-tu-vo cha-yi-nu.

Praised be (*if ten or more are present*, our God,) the One of whose bounty we have eaten and through whose goodness we survive.

Leader

בָּרוּךְ הוּא וּבָרוּךְ שְׁמוֹ:

Ba-ruch hu u-va-ruch she-mo!

Praised be You! Praised be Your Name!

(An Alternative Birkat Ha-Mazon will be found on page 90.)

THE FIRST BLESSING: For Food

All

בָּרוּךְ אַתָּה יְיָ אֱלֹהֵינוּ מֶלֶךְ הָעוֹלָם הַזָּן אֶת־הָעוֹלָם כֻּלּוֹ
בְּטוּבוֹ בְּחֵן בְּחֶסֶד וּבְרַחֲמִים הוּא נוֹתֵן לֶחֶם לְכָל־בָּשָׂר
כִּי לְעוֹלָם חַסְדּוֹ: וּבְטוּבוֹ הַגָּדוֹל תָּמִיד לֹא־חָסַר לָנוּ
וְאַל יֶחְסַר לָנוּ מָזוֹן לְעוֹלָם וָעֶד. בַּעֲבוּר שְׁמוֹ הַגָּדוֹל. כִּי
הוּא אֵל זָן וּמְפַרְנֵס לַכֹּל וּמֵטִיב לַכֹּל וּמֵכִין מָזוֹן לְכָל
בְּרִיּוֹתָיו אֲשֶׁר בָּרָא. בָּרוּךְ אַתָּה יְיָ הַזָּן אֶת־הַכֹּל:

Ba-ruch a-ta A-do-nai, E-lo-hei-nu me-lech ha-o-lam,
ha-zan et ha-o-lam ku-lo be-tu-vo, be-chen be-che-sed
u-ve-ra-cha-mim. Hu no-ten le-chem le-chol ba-sar, ki
le-o-lam chas-do, u-ve-tu-vo ha-ga-dol ta-mid lo cha-sar
la-nu, ve-al yech-sar la-nu ma-zon le-o-lam va-ed, ba-a-
vur she-mo ha-ga-dol, ki hu El zan u-me-far-nes la-kol,
u-me-tiv la-kol u-me-chin ma-zon le-chol bri-o-tav
a-sher ba-ra. Ba-ruch a-ta A-do-nai, ha-zan et ha-kol.

You are praised, Adonai our God,
Ruler of time and space,
Who feeds the world,
All the world,
With goodness and grace, love and compassion.
You give bread to all flesh,
For the love with which You sealed Your covenant with
    humanity
Is eternal.
Because of Your great goodness,
Your great Name,
There is no lack of food for us,
There should never be any lack of food for us,
For You are a God who feeds and sustains all life,
Who does good for all things,
Who prepares food for all Your creatures
Whom You created.
You are praised, Adonai our God,
Who feeds all life.

THE SECOND BLESSING: For the Land

נוֹדֶה לְךָ יְיָ אֱלֹהֵינוּ עַל שֶׁהִנְחַלְתָּ לַאֲבוֹתֵינוּ
(וּלְאִמּוֹתֵינוּ) אֶרֶץ חֶמְדָּה טוֹבָה וּרְחָבָה. וְעַל
שֶׁהוֹצֵאתָנוּ יְיָ אֱלֹהֵינוּ מֵאֶרֶץ מִצְרַיִם וּפְדִיתָנוּ מִבֵּית
עֲבָדִים. וְעַל בְּרִיתְךָ שֶׁחָתַמְתָּ בִּבְשָׂרֵנוּ (וּבְלִבֵּנוּ) וְעַל
תּוֹרָתְךָ שֶׁלִּמַּדְתָּנוּ וְעַל חֻקֶּיךָ שֶׁהוֹדַעְתָּנוּ. וְעַל חַיִּים חֵן
וָחֶסֶד שֶׁחוֹנַנְתָּנוּ. וְעַל אֲכִילַת מָזוֹן שָׁאַתָּה זָן וּמְפַרְנֵס
אוֹתָנוּ תָּמִיד בְּכָל־יוֹם וּבְכָל־עֵת וּבְכָל־שָׁעָה:

No-deh le-cha A-do-nai E-lo-hei-nu al she-hin-chal-ta
la-a-vo-tei-nu (u-le-i-mo-tei-nu) e-retz chem-da to-va
u-re-cha-va, ve-al she-ho-tzei-ta-nu A-do-nai E-lo-hei-
nu me-e-retz Mitz-ra-yim u-fe-di-ta-nu mi-beit a-va-
dim, ve-al be-rit-cha she-cha-tam-ta bi-ve-sa-re-nu
(u-ve-li-be-nu), ve al To-rat-cha she-li-mad-ta-nu, ve-al
chu-ke-cha she-ho-da-ta-nu, ve-al cha-yim chen va-che-
sed she-cho-nan-ta-nu, ve-al a-chi-lat ma-zon sha-a-ta
zan u-me-far-nes o-ta-nu ta-mid, be-chol yom u-ve-chol
et u-ve-chol sha-ah.

We thank You, Adonai our God, for bestowing on our
fathers and mothers a pleasant land, good and broad, for
bringing us out of the narrow land of Mitzrayim, ransoming
us from the house of slaves; and for Your covenant that You
have sealed in our flesh (and on our heart); for Your Torah
which You Yourself have taught us; for Your ancient laws
that You have revealed to us; for life and grace and covenantal love which You have graciously given us; and for the eating of food with which You feed and sustain us always, every
day, every season, every hour.

וְעַל הַכֹּל יְיָ אֱלֹהֵינוּ אֲנַחְנוּ מוֹדִים לָךְ וּמְבָרְכִים אוֹתָךְ
יִתְבָּרַךְ שִׁמְךָ בְּפִי כָל־חַי תָּמִיד לְעוֹלָם וָעֶד: כַּכָּתוּב
וְאָכַלְתָּ וְשָׂבָעְתָּ וּבֵרַכְתָּ אֶת־יְיָ אֱלֹהֶיךָ עַל־הָאָרֶץ הַטֹּבָה
אֲשֶׁר נָתַן־לָךְ. בָּרוּךְ אַתָּה יְיָ עַל־הָאָרֶץ וְעַל־הַמָּזוֹן:

Ve-al ha-kol A-do-nai E-lo-hei-nu a-nach-nu mo-dim lach, u-me-va-re-chim o-tach, yit-ba-rach shim-cha be-fi chol chai ta-mid le-o-lam va-ed. Ka-ka-tuv: ve-a-chal-ta ve-sa-va-ta u-ve-rach-ta et A-do-nai E-lo-he-cha al ha-a-retz ha-to-va a-sher na-tan lach. Ba-ruch a-ta A-do-nai, al ha-a-retz ve-al ha-ma-zon.

For everything, Adonai our God, we thank You and praise You—how praiseworthy is Your Name forever, in every place, at every moment, in the mouth of everything that lives! As it is written (Deuteronomy 8:10): "And you shall eat and you shall be satisfied and you shall praise Adonai your God for the good land which God has given you." You are praised, Adonai, for the land and for food.

THE THIRD BLESSING: For Sustenance

רַחֶם יְיָ אֱלֹהֵינוּ עַל־יִשְׂרָאֵל עַמֶּךְ וְעַל־יְרוּשָׁלַיִם עִירֶךְ וְעַל צִיּוֹן מִשְׁכַּן כְּבוֹדֶךְ וְעַל־מַלְכוּת בֵּית דָּוִד מְשִׁיחֶךְ וְעַל־הַבַּיִת הַגָּדוֹל וְהַקָּדוֹשׁ שֶׁנִּקְרָא שִׁמְךָ עָלָיו: אֱלֹהֵינוּ אָבִינוּ רְעֵנוּ זוּנֵנוּ פַּרְנְסֵנוּ וְכַלְכְּלֵנוּ וְהַרְוִיחֵנוּ וְהַרְוַח־לָנוּ יְיָ אֱלֹהֵינוּ מְהֵרָה מִכָּל־צָרוֹתֵינוּ: וְנָא אַל־תַּצְרִיכֵנוּ יְיָ אֱלֹהֵינוּ לֹא לִידֵי מַתְּנַת בָּשָׂר וָדָם וְלֹא לִידֵי הַלְוָאָתָם. כִּי־אִם לְיָדְךָ הַמְּלֵאָה הַפְּתוּחָה הַקְּדוֹשָׁה וְהָרְחָבָה שֶׁלֹּא נֵבוֹשׁ וְלֹא נִכָּלֵם לְעוֹלָם וָעֶד:

Ra-chem A-do-nai E-lo-hei-nu al Yis-ra-el a-me-cha ve-al Ye-ru-sha-la-yim i-re-cha ve-al Tzi-yon mish-kan ke-vo-de-cha ve-al mal-chut beit Da-vid me-shi-che-cha ve-al ha-ba-yit ha-ga-dol ve-ha-ka-dosh she-nik-ra shim-cha a-lav. E-lo-hei-nu a-vi-nu re-ei-nu zu-nei-nu par-ne-sei-nu ve-chal-ke-lei-nu ve-har-vi-chei-nu ve-har-vach la-nu A-do-nai E-lo-hei-nu me-hei-ra mi-kol tza-ro-tei-nu. Ve-na al tatz-ri-chei-nu A-do-nai E-lo-hei-nu lo li-dei mat-nat ba-sar va-dam ve-lo li-dei hal-va-a-tam, ki im le-yad-cha ha-me-lei-ah ha-pe-tu-cha ha-ke-do-sha ve-ha-re-cha-va, she-lo ne-vosh ve-lo ni-ka-lem le-o-lam va-ed.

Shed compassion over this people Israel that You created, Adonai our God: over Jerusalem, Your own city; over Zion, the resting place of Your glory; over the realm of the house of David, Your anointed messiah; and over the great and holy House over which Your Name is spoken. Our God, our Father and our Mother, shepherd us, feed us, nurture us, sustain us, relieve us, grant us relief soon, Adonai our God, from all our sorrows! And pray, do not make us dependent on the hand of other people, through gifts or loans, but only on Your hand, full and open, holy and generous, that we might never be disgraced or degraded at any time, in any place.

INSERTION: A Shabbat Prayer
[To Be Said on Friday Night]

[רְצֵה וְהַחֲלִיצֵנוּ יְיָ אֱלֹהֵינוּ בְּמִצְוֹתֶיךָ וּבְמִצְוַת יוֹם
הַשְּׁבִיעִי הַשַּׁבָּת הַגָּדוֹל וְהַקָּדוֹשׁ הַזֶּה כִּי יוֹם זֶה גָּדוֹל
וְקָדוֹשׁ הוּא לְפָנֶיךָ לִשְׁבָּת־בּוֹ וְלָנוּחַ בּוֹ בְּאַהֲבָה כְּמִצְוַת
רְצוֹנֶךָ: וּבִרְצוֹנְךָ הָנִיחַ לָנוּ יְיָ אֱלֹהֵינוּ שֶׁלֹּא תְהֵא צָרָה
וְיָגוֹן וַאֲנָחָה בְּיוֹם מְנוּחָתֵינוּ. וְהַרְאֵנוּ יְיָ אֱלֹהֵינוּ בְּנֶחָמַת
צִיּוֹן עִירֶךָ וּבְבִנְיַן יְרוּשָׁלַיִם עִיר קָדְשֶׁךָ. כִּי אַתָּה הוּא
בַּעַל הַיְשׁוּעוֹת וּבַעַל הַנֶּחָמוֹת:]

[Re-tzei ve-ha-cha-li-tzei-nu A-do-nai E-lo-hei-nu be-mitz-vo-te-cha u-ve-mitz-vat yom ha-she-vi-i ha-Sha-bat ha-ga-dol ve-ha-ka-dosh ha-zeh. Ki yom zeh ga-dol ve-ka-dosh hu le-fa-ne-cha, lish-bot bo ve-la-nu-ach bo be-a-ha-va ke-mitz-vat re-tzo-ne-cha, u-vir-tzon-cha ha-ni-ach la-nu A-do-nai E-lo-hei-nu she-lo te-hei tza-ra ve-ya-gon va-a-na-cha be-yom me-nu-cha-tei-nu, ve-har-ei-nu A-do-nai E-lo-hei-nu be-ne-cha-mat Tzi-yon i-re-cha u-ve-vin-yan Ye-ru-sha-la-yim ir kod-she-cha ki a-ta hu ba-al ha-ye-shu-ot u-va-al ha-ne-cha-mot.]

[Favor us with a mind at peace, Adonai our God, as we strive to fulfill Your mitzvot, especially the mitzvah of the Seventh Day, Shabbat, so grand and holy. For this grand

and holy day exists in Your presence, lovingly to cease work and to rest, according to the mitzvah with which You have favored us. For through Your favor, Adonai our God, it has given us rest, that there might be no sorrow, no pain, no grief, on this day of our rest. Instead, Adonai our God, show us the comforting of Zion Your city and the rebuilding of Jerusalem Your holy city, for You are the source of victory over all enemies, You are the source of comfort.]

INSERTION: A Festival Prayer (Ya-a-leh Ve-ya-vo)
(To Be Said Every Night in Passover)

אֱלֹהֵינוּ וֵאלֹהֵי אֲבוֹתֵינוּ (וְאִמּוֹתֵינוּ). יַעֲלֶה וְיָבֹא וְיַגִּיעַ
וְיֵרָאֶה וְיֵרָצֶה וְיִשָּׁמַע וְיִפָּקֵד וְיִזָּכֵר זִכְרוֹנֵנוּ וּפִקְדּוֹנֵנוּ.
וְזִכְרוֹן אֲבוֹתֵינוּ (וְאִמּוֹתֵינוּ). וְזִכְרוֹן מָשִׁיחַ בֶּן דָּוִד
עַבְדֶּךָ. וְזִכְרוֹן יְרוּשָׁלַיִם עִיר קָדְשֶׁךָ. וְזִכְרוֹן כָּל־עַמְּךָ
בֵּית יִשְׂרָאֵל לְפָנֶיךָ. לִפְלֵיטָה לְטוֹבָה לְחֵן וּלְחֶסֶד
וּלְרַחֲמִים לְחַיִּים וּלְשָׁלוֹם בְּיוֹם חַג הַמַּצּוֹת הַזֶּה. זָכְרֵנוּ
יְיָ אֱלֹהֵינוּ בּוֹ לְטוֹבָה. וּפָקְדֵנוּ בוֹ לִבְרָכָה. וְהוֹשִׁיעֵנוּ בוֹ
לְחַיִּים. וּבִדְבַר יְשׁוּעָה וְרַחֲמִים חוּס וְחָנֵּנוּ. וְרַחֵם עָלֵינוּ
וְהוֹשִׁיעֵנוּ. כִּי אֵלֶיךָ עֵינֵינוּ. כִּי אֵל מֶלֶךְ חַנּוּן וְרַחוּם
אָתָּה:

E-lo-hei-nu vE-lo-hei a-vo-tei-nu (ve-i-mo-tei-nu), ya-a-leh ve-ya-vo ve-ya-gi-a ve-yei-ra-eh ve-yei-ra-tzeh ve-yi-sha-ma ve-yi-pa-ked ve-yi-za-cher zich-ro-nei-nu u-fik-do-nei-nu, ve-zich-ron a-vo-tei-nu (ve-i-mo-tei-nu), ve-zich-ron ma-shi-ach ben Da-vid ave-de-cha, ve-zich-ron Ye-ru-sha-la-yim ir kod-she-cha, ve-zich-ron kol am-cha beit Yis-ra-el le-fa-ne-cha, lif-lei-ta le-to-vah le-chen u-le-che-sed u-le-ra-cha-mim, le-cha-yim u-le-sha-lom be-yom Chag Ha-Ma-tzot ha-zeh. Zoch-rei-nu A-do-nai E-lo-hei-nu bo le-to-vah, u-fok-dei-nu vo liv-ra-cha, ve-ho-shi-ei-nu vo le-cha-yim. U-vi-de-var ye-shu-a ve-ra-cha-mim chus ve-chawn-nei-nu ve-ra-chem a-lei-nu ve-ho-shi-ei-nu, ki ei-le-cha ei-nei-nu, ki El me-lech cha-nun ve-ra-chum a-ta.

Our God, God of our fathers and mothers,
May there ascend and enter and approach and be seen and be
favored and be heard and be assembled and be
presented:
Our presence and our gathering,
The presence of our fathers and mothers,
The presence of Your servant the Messiah, child of David,
The presence of Jerusalem Your holy city,
The presence of all Your people the House of Israel,
Before You
With prayers for rescue, for good, for grace, for love, for
compassion, for life, and for peace,
On this day of the Matzah Festival.
May we be present for good,
Assemble us for blessing,
Bring us the victorious reward of a good life.

And with a promise of righteous victory and compassion,
spare us, grace us, be compassionate with us, and bring us
the victory of the righteous, for our eyes turn to You, God
and monarch, *Chanun ve-Rachum*, Source of grace and
compassion.

THE THIRD BLESSING CONCLUDED:
A Prayer for Jerusalem

וּבְנֵה יְרוּשָׁלַיִם עִיר הַקֹּדֶשׁ בִּמְהֵרָה בְיָמֵינוּ: בָּרוּךְ אַתָּה
יְיָ. בּוֹנֶה בְרַחֲמָיו יְרוּשָׁלָיִם. אָמֵן:

U-ve-nei Ye-ru-sha-la-yim ir ha-ko-desh bim-hei-ra ve-
ya-mei-nu. Ba-ruch a-ta A-do-nai, bo-neh ve-ra-cha-mav
Ye-ru-sha-la-yim, a-men.

And rebuild Jerusalem, Your holy city, quickly, while we are
still alive. You are praised, Adonai, who with compassion is
rebuilding Jerusalem.

Amen.

THE FOURTH BLESSING: For Good

בָּרוּךְ אַתָּה יְיָ אֱלֹהֵינוּ מֶלֶךְ הָעוֹלָם. הָאֵל אָבִינוּ מַלְכֵּנוּ
אַדִּירֵנוּ בּוֹרְאֵנוּ גֹּאֲלֵנוּ יוֹצְרֵנוּ קְדוֹשֵׁנוּ קְדוֹשׁ יַעֲקֹב
רוֹעֵנוּ רוֹעֵה יִשְׂרָאֵל הַמֶּלֶךְ הַטּוֹב וְהַמֵּטִיב לַכֹּל שֶׁבְּכָל
יוֹם וָיוֹם הוּא הֵטִיב הוּא מֵטִיב הוּא יֵיטִיב לָנוּ: הוּא
גְמָלָנוּ הוּא גוֹמְלֵנוּ הוּא יִגְמְלֵנוּ לָעַד לְחֵן לְחֶסֶד
וּלְרַחֲמִים וּלְרֶוַח הַצָּלָה וְהַצְלָחָה בְּרָכָה וִישׁוּעָה נֶחָמָה
פַּרְנָסָה וְכַלְכָּלָה וְרַחֲמִים וְחַיִּים וְשָׁלוֹם וְכָל־טוֹב וּמִכָּל־
טוֹב לְעוֹלָם אַל יְחַסְּרֵנוּ:

Ba-ruch a-ta A-do-nai E-lo-hei-nu me-lech ha-o-lam,
ha-El a-vi-nu mal-kei-nu a-di-rei-nu bor-ei-nu go-a-lei-
nu yotz-rei-nu ke-do-shei-nu ke-dosh Ya-a-kov. Ro-ei-
nu ro-ei Yis-ra-el, ha-me-lech ha-tov ve-ha-mei-tiv
la-kol, she-be-chol yom va-yom hu hei-tiv hu mei-tiv hu
yei-tiv la-nu, hu ge-ma-la-nu hu gom-lei-nu hu yig-me-
lei-nu la-ad, le-chen le-che-sed u-le-ra-cha-mim u-le-re-
vach ha-tza-la ve-hatz-la-cha be-ra-cha vi-shu-a ne-
cha-ma par-na-sa ve-chal-ka-la, ve-ra-cha-mim ve-cha-
yim ve-sha-lom ve-chol tov, u-mi-kol tov le-o-lam al
ye-chas-rei-nu.

You are praised, Adonai our God, ruler over time and space,
God our Motherfather, our Sovereign, our Might, our
Creator, our Redeemer, our Shaper, Source of our holiness,
Holy One of Jacob, our Shepherd, Shepherd of Israel, Sovereign who is good and does good for all. Every single day You
have done good, You do good, and may You continue to do
good for us. You have been kind to us, You are kind to us,
and may You continue to be kind to us, showing us grace
and love, compassion and redress, salvation and success,
blessing and righteous victory, comfort, sustenance and support, compassion, long life and peace, and every goodness.
May no goodness ever be lacking from us.

CONCLUDING PRAYERS

הָרַחֲמָן הוּא יִמְלוֹךְ עָלֵינוּ לְעוֹלָם וָעֶד:

Ha-ra-cha-man hu yim-loch a-lei-nu le-o-lam va-ed.

May the Compassionate One rule over us always, wherever we may be!

הָרַחֲמָן הוּא יִתְבָּרַךְ בַּשָּׁמַיִם וּבָאָרֶץ:

Ha-ra-cha-man hu yit-ba-rach ba-sha-ma-yim u-va-a-retz.

May the Compassionate One be praised in the heavens and on earth!

הָרַחֲמָן הוּא יִשְׁתַּבַּח לְדוֹר דּוֹרִים וְיִתְפָּאַר־בָּנוּ לָנֶצַח נְצָחִים וְיִתְהַדַּר־בָּנוּ לָעַד וּלְעוֹלְמֵי עוֹלָמִים:

Ha-ra-cha-man hu yish-ta-bach le-dor do-rim, ve-yit-pa-ar ba-nu le-ne-tzach ne-tza-chim, ve-yit-ha-dar ba-nu la-ad u-le-ol-mei o-la-mim.

May the Compassionate One be hailed in every generation, glorified through us forever until eternity, adorned by us forever, until the end of time!

הָרַחֲמָן הוּא יְפַרְנְסֵנוּ בְּכָבוֹד:

Ha-ra-cha-man hu ye-far-ne-sei-nu be-cha-vod.

May the Compassionate One sustain us honorably.

הָרַחֲמָן הוּא יִשְׁבּוֹר עֻלֵּנוּ מֵעַל צַוָּארֵנוּ וְהוּא יוֹלִיכֵנוּ קוֹמְמִיּוּת לְאַרְצֵנוּ:

Ha-ra-cha-man hu yish-bor u-lei-nu me-al tza-va-rei-nu, ve-hu yo-li-che-nu ko-me-mi-yut le-ar-tzei-nu.

May the Compassionate One break the yoke that bends our neck, and bring us walking upright into our land.

הָרַחֲמָן הוּא יִשְׁלַח בְּרָכָה מְרֻבָּה בַּבַּיִת הַזֶּה וְעַל שֻׁלְחָן זֶה שֶׁאָכַלְנוּ עָלָיו:

Ha-ra-cha-man hu yish-lach be-ra-cha me-ru-ba ba-ba-yit ha-zeh ve-al shul-chan zeh she-a-chal-nu a-lav.

May the Compassionate One send bountiful blessings to this house and upon this table on which we have eaten.

הָרַחֲמָן הוּא יִשְׁלַח־לָנוּ אֶת־אֵלִיָּהוּ הַנָּבִיא זָכוּר לַטּוֹב וִיבַשֶּׂר־לָנוּ בְּשׂוֹרוֹת טוֹבוֹת יְשׁוּעוֹת וְנֶחָמוֹת:

Ha-ra-cha-man hu yish-lach la-nu et E-li-ya-hu ha-na-vi za-chur la-tov, vi-va-ser la-nu be-so-rot to-vot ye-shu-ot ve-ne-cha-mot.

May the Compassionate One send us Eliyahu ha-Navi, Elijah the Prophet, who is remembered for all his goodness! May he bestow on us the good news of righteous victories and messianic consolations.

A Woman Says:

הָרַחֲמָן הוּא יְבָרֵךְ אוֹתִי (וְאֶת־אִישִׁי) (וְאֶת־זַרְעִי) וְאֶת־כָּל־אֲשֶׁר לִי.

Ha-ra-cha-man hu ye-va-rech o-ti (ve-et i-shi) (ve-et zar-i) ve-et kol a-sher li.

May the Compassionate One bless me (and my husband) (and our children) and all my family.

A Man Says:

הָרַחֲמָן הוּא יְבָרֵךְ אוֹתִי (וְאֶת־אִשְׁתִּי) (וְאֶת־זַרְעִי) וְאֶת־כָּל־אֲשֶׁר לִי.

Ha-ra-cha-man hu ye-va-rech o-ti (ve-et ish-ti) (ve-et zar-i) ve-et kol a-sher li.

May the Compassionate One bless me (and my wife) (and our children) and all my family.

Those Dining in Their Parents' Home Say:

הָרַחֲמָן הוּא יְבָרֵךְ אֶת־אָבִי מוֹרִי בַּעַל הַבַּיִת הַזֶּה וְאֶת־
אִמִּי מוֹרָתִי בַּעֲלַת הַבַּיִת הַזֶּה אוֹתָם וְאֶת־בֵּיתָם וְאֶת־
זַרְעָם וְאֶת־כָּל־אֲשֶׁר לָהֶם.

Ha-ra-cha-man hu ye-va-rech et a-vi mo-ri ba-al ha-ba-yit ha-zeh ve-et i-mi mo-ra-ti ba-a-lat ha-ba-yit ha-zeh, o-tam ve-et bei-tam ve-et zar-am ve-et kol a-sher la-hem.

May the Compassionate One bless my father and mother, my teachers, who guide this household, they and all who dwell here, their children, and all they have.

Guests in a Home Say:

הָרַחֲמָן הוּא יְבָרֵךְ אֶת־בַּעַל הַבַּיִת הַזֶּה וְאֶת בַּעֲלַת
הַבַּיִת הַזֶּה אוֹתָם וְאֶת־בֵּיתָם וְאֶת־זַרְעָם וְאֶת־כָּל־אֲשֶׁר
לָהֶם.

Ha-ra-cha-man hu ye-va-rech et ba-al ha-ba-yit ha-zeh ve-et ba-a-lat ha-ba-yit ha-zeh, o-tam ve-et bei-tam ve-et zar-am ve-et kol a-sher la-hem.

May the Compassionate One bless those who guide this household, they and all who dwell here, their children, and all they have.

Participants in a Public Seder Say:

הָרַחֲמָן הוּא יְבָרֵךְ אֶת־כָּל־הַמְסֻבִּין כָּאן.

Ha-ra-cha-man hu ye-va-rech et kol ha-me-su-bin kan.

May the Compassionate One bless all who are dining here.

All Say:

אוֹתָנוּ וְאֶת־כָּל־אֲשֶׁר לָנוּ, כְּמוֹ שֶׁנִּתְבָּרְכוּ (אִמּוֹתֵינוּ
שָׂרָה רִבְקָה רָחֵל וְלֵאָה וְ) אֲבוֹתֵינוּ אַבְרָהָם יִצְחָק

וְיַעֲקֹב בַּכֹּל מִכֹּל כֹּל. כֵּן יְבָרֵךְ אוֹתָנוּ כֻּלָּנוּ יַחַד בִּבְרָכָה שְׁלֵמָה וְנֹאמַר אָמֵן:

O-ta-nu ve-et kol a-sher la-nu, ke-mo she-nit-ba-re-chu (i-mo-tei-nu Sa-rah, Riv-kah, Ra-chel ve-Le-ah, ve-) a-vo-tei-nu Av-ra-ham, Yitz-chak, ve-Ya-a-kov, ba-kol, mi-kol, kol. Ken ye-va-rech o-ta-nu ku-la-nu ya-chad biv-ra-cha she-lei-ma, ve-no-mar a-men.

May God bless all of us and all that belong to us, as You blessed (our mothers Sarah, Rebecca, Rachel, and Leah, and) our fathers Abraham, "with all" (Genesis 24:1), Isaac, "from all" (Genesis 26:33), and Jacob, "all" (Genesis 33:11). So may God bless us all together, with a blessing of complete harmony, and let us say: Amen.

בַּמָּרוֹם יְלַמְּדוּ עֲלֵיהֶם וְעָלֵינוּ זְכוּת שֶׁתְּהִי לְמִשְׁמֶרֶת שָׁלוֹם. וְנִשָּׂא בְרָכָה מֵאֵת יְיָ וּצְדָקָה מֵאֱלֹהֵי יִשְׁעֵנוּ: וְנִמְצָא־חֵן וְשֵׂכֶל טוֹב בְּעֵינֵי אֱלֹהִים וְאָדָם:

Ba-ma-rom ye-la-me-du a-lei-hem ve-a-lei-nu ze-chut she-te-hi le-mish-me-ret sha-lom, ve-ni-sa ve-ra-cha me-et A-do-nai u-tze-da-ka mei-E-lo-hei yish-ei-nu, ve-nim-tza chen ve-se-chel tov be-ei-nei E-lo-him ve-a-dam.

May our merit be expounded on high, that it might safeguard our peace and welfare. Let a divine blessing be raised for us, and justice from the God who gives righteous victories. May we find grace and good understanding in the eyes of God and humanity.

[On Friday Night add:]

[הָרַחֲמָן הוּא יַנְחִילֵנוּ יוֹם שֶׁכֻּלּוֹ שַׁבָּת וּמְנוּחָה לְחַיֵּי הָעוֹלָמִים:]

[Ha-ra-cha-man hu yan-chi-lei-nu yom she-ku-lo Sha-bat, u-me-nu-cha le-cha-yei ha-o-la-mim.]

[May the Compassionate One bestow on us a day of total Sabbath, filled with the restfulness of the life to come.]

(On the First Two Nights Add:)

(הָרַחֲמָן הוּא יַנְחִילֵנוּ יוֹם שֶׁכֻּלוֹ טוֹב:)

(Ha-ra-cha-man hu yan-chi-lei-nu yom she-ku-lo tov.)

(May the Compassionate One bestow on us a day that is a complete festival of goodness.)

הָרַחֲמָן הוּא יְזַכֵּנוּ לִימוֹת הַמָּשִׁיחַ וּלְחַיֵּי הָעוֹלָם הַבָּא:

Ha-ra-cha-man hu ye-za-kei-nu li-mot ha-ma-shi-ach u-le-cha-yei ha-o-lam ha-ba.

May the Compassionate One let us merit seeing the days of the Messiah and the life of the World to Come.

מִגְדּוֹל יְשׁוּעוֹת מַלְכּוֹ וְעֹשֶׂה חֶסֶד לִמְשִׁיחוֹ לְדָוִד וּלְזַרְעוֹ עַד־עוֹלָם. עֹשֶׂה שָׁלוֹם בִּמְרוֹמָיו הוּא יַעֲשֶׂה שָׁלוֹם עָלֵינוּ וְעַל־כָּל־יִשְׂרָאֵל וְאִמְרוּ אָמֵן:

Mig-dol ye-shu-ot mal-ko ve-o-seh che-sed lim-shi-cho le-Da-vid u-le-zar-o ad o-lam. O-seh sha-lom bim-ro-mav hu ya-a-seh sha-lom a-lei-nu ve-al kol Yis-ra-el, ve-im-ru a-men.

God is a tower of righteous victories for the one who rules in God's name, an eternal Provider of covenantal love for the one God has anointed, David and his seed. May the One who makes peace in the high places make peace over us and over all Israel. Amen.

יְראוּ אֶת־יְיָ קְדֹשָׁיו כִּי אֵין מַחְסוֹר לִירֵאָיו: כְּפִירִים רָשׁוּ וְרָעֵבוּ וְדֹרְשֵׁי יְיָ לֹא־יַחְסְרוּ כָל־טוֹב: הוֹדוּ לַייָ כִּי־טוֹב כִּי לְעוֹלָם חַסְדּוֹ: פּוֹתֵחַ אֶת־יָדֶךָ וּמַשְׂבִּיעַ לְכָל־חַי רָצוֹן: בָּרוּךְ הַגֶּבֶר אֲשֶׁר יִבְטַח בַּייָ וְהָיָה יְיָ מִבְטַחוֹ: נַעַר הָיִיתִי גַּם־זָקַנְתִּי וְלֹא־רָאִיתִי צַדִּיק נֶעֱזָב וְזַרְעוֹ מְבַקֶּשׁ לָחֶם: יְיָ עֹז לְעַמּוֹ יִתֵּן יְיָ יְבָרֵךְ אֶת־עַמּוֹ בַשָּׁלוֹם:

Yer-u et A-do-nai ke-do-shav ki ein mach-sor li-rei-av.
Ke-fi-rim ra-shu ve-ra-ei-vu ve-dor-shei A-do-nai lo
yach-se-ru chol tov. Ho-du lA-do-nai ki tov, ki-le-o-lam
chas-do, po-te-ach et ya-de-cha u-mas-bi-a le-chol chai
ra-tzon. Ba-ruch ha-ge-ver a-sher yiv-tach bA-do-nai,
ve-ha-ya A-do-nai miv-ta-cho. Na-ar ha-yi-ti, gam za-
kan-ti, ve-lo ra-i-ti tza-dik ne-e-zav ve-zar-o me-va-kesh
la-chem. A-do-nai oz le-a-mo yi-ten, A-do-nai ye-va-
rech et a-mo va-sha-lom.

Revere Adonai, O holy ones, for nothing is lacking to those
who revere the Eternal.
Young lions are ever ravenous, but those who seek Adonai
lack nothing of the good.
Give thanks to Adonai who is good, whose love is eternal,
Opening Your hand and giving every living thing the satis-
faction of Your favor.
Blessed is the person who trusts in Adonai, whose reliance is
on God;
A youth was I, and even as I age, never have I seen a righteous person really abandoned, with children begging
for bread.
Adonai, You give strength to Your people. May You ever
bless Your people with peace.

(Continue with the Third Cup on page 94.)

ALTERNATIVE BIRKAT HA-MAZON

(On Shabbat and festivals, Psalm 126, Shir Ha-Ma-a-lot (page 76) is
offered before Birkat Ha-Mazon. Zimun, the Invitation, is found on
page 77.)

THE FIRST BLESSING: For Food

בָּרוּךְ אַתָּה יְיָ אֱלֹהֵינוּ מֶלֶךְ הָעוֹלָם הַזָּן אֶת־הָעוֹלָם כֻּלּוֹ
בְּטוּבוֹ בְּחֵן בְּחֶסֶד וּבְרַחֲמִים הוּא נוֹתֵן לֶחֶם לְכָל־בָּשָׂר
כִּי לְעוֹלָם חַסְדּוֹ: וּבְטוּבוֹ הַגָּדוֹל תָּמִיד לֹא־חָסַר לָנוּ

וְאַל יֶחְסַר לָנוּ מָזוֹן לְעוֹלָם וָעֶד. בַּעֲבוּר שְׁמוֹ הַגָּדוֹל. כִּי הוּא אֵל זָן וּמְפַרְנֵס לַכֹּל וּמֵטִיב לַכֹּל וּמֵכִין מָזוֹן לְכָל בְּרִיּוֹתָיו אֲשֶׁר בָּרָא. בָּרוּךְ אַתָּה יְיָ הַזָּן אֶת־הַכֹּל:

Ba-ruch a-ta A-do-nai, E-lo-hei-nu me-lech ha-o-lam, ha-zan et ha-o-lam ku-lo be-tu-vo, be-chen be-che-sed u-ve-ra-cha-mim. Hu no-ten le-chem le-chol ba-sar, ki le-o-lam chas-do, u-ve-tu-vo ha-ga-dol ta-mid lo cha-sar la-nu, ve-al yech-sar la-nu ma-zon le-o-lam va-ed, ba-a-vur she-mo ha-ga-dol, ki hu El zan u-me-far-nes la-kol, u-me-tiv la-kol u-me-chin ma-zon le-chol be-ri-o-tav a-sher ba-ra. Ba-ruch a-ta A-do-nai, ha-zan et ha-kol.

You are praised, Adonai our God,
Ruler of time and space,
Who feeds the world,
All the world,
With goodness and grace, love and compassion.
You give bread to all flesh,
For the love with which You sealed Your covenant with
    humanity
Is eternal.
Because of Your great goodness,
Your great Name,
There is no lack of food for us,
There should never be any lack of food for us,
For You are a God who feeds and sustains all life,
Who does good for all things,
Who prepares food for all Your creatures
Whom You created.
You are praised, Adonai our God,
Who feeds all life.

Help us learn from You
How to feed the hungry
And carry out Your plan
That all creatures are to be fed and sustained,
With none on earth having more than they need,
Or less.

THE SECOND BLESSING: For the Land

וְעַל הַכֹּל יְיָ אֱלֹהֵינוּ אֲנַחְנוּ מוֹדִים לָךְ וּמְבָרְכִים אוֹתָךְ
יִתְבָּרַךְ שִׁמְךָ בְּפִי כָל־חַי תָּמִיד לְעוֹלָם וָעֶד: כַּכָּתוּב
וְאָכַלְתָּ וְשָׂבָעְתָּ וּבֵרַכְתָּ אֶת־יְיָ אֱלֹהֶיךָ עַל־הָאָרֶץ הַטֹּבָה
אֲשֶׁר נָתַן־לָךְ. בָּרוּךְ אַתָּה יְיָ עַל־הָאָרֶץ וְעַל־הַמָּזוֹן:

Ve-al ha-kol A-do-nai E-lo-hei-nu a-nach-nu mo-dim
lach, u-me-va-re-chim o-tach, yit-ba-rach shim-cha be-fi
chol chai ta-mid le-o-lam va-ed. Ka-ka-tuv: ve-a-chal-ta
ve-sa-va-ta u-vei-rach-ta et A-do-nai E-lo-he-cha al
ha-a-retz ha-to-va a-sher na-tan lach. Ba-ruch a-ta
A-do-nai, al ha-a-retz ve-al ha-ma-zon.

For everything, Adonai our God, we thank You and praise
You—how praiseworthy is Your Name forever, in every
place, at every moment, in the mouth of everything that
lives! As it is written: "And you shall eat and you shall be
satisfied, and you shall praise Adonai your God for the good
land which God has given you" (Deuteronomy 8:10). You
are praised, Adonai, for the land and for food.

THE THIRD BLESSING: For Sustenance

Shed compassion over this people Israel that You created,
Adonai our God, and over Jerusalem, Your own city. O God,
humanity tonight is like a band of errant slaves, newly freed.
Shepherd us, nurture us, sustain us, grant us relief soon
from all our sorrows.

INSERTION: A Shabbat Prayer
[To Be Said on Friday Night]

[Favor us with a mind at peace, Adonai our God, as we strive
to fulfill Your mitzvot, and especially the mitzvah of the
Seventh Day, Shabbat, so grand and holy.]

INSERTION: A Festival Prayer
(To Be Said Every Night in Passover)

Our God and God of our fathers and mothers, on this day of the Matzah Festival may we be present for good. Assemble us for blessing, bring us the victorious reward of a good life. Our eyes turn to You, God and Monarch, *Chanun ve-Rachum*, Source of grace and compassion.

THE THIRD BLESSING CONCLUDED:
A Prayer for Jerusalem

וּבְנֵה יְרוּשָׁלַיִם עִיר הַקֹּדֶשׁ בִּמְהֵרָה בְיָמֵינוּ: בָּרוּךְ אַתָּה
יְיָ. בּוֹנֵה בְרַחֲמָיו יְרוּשָׁלַיִם. אָמֵן:

U-ve-nei Ye-ru-sha-la-yim ir ha-ko-desh bim-hei-ra ve-ya-mei-nu. Ba-ruch a-ta A-do-nai, bo-neh ve-ra-cha-mav Ye-ru-sha-la-yim, a-men.

And rebuild Jerusalem, Your holy city, quickly, while we are still alive. You are praised, Adonai, who with compassion is rebuilding Jerusalem. Amen.

THE FOURTH BLESSING: For Good

You are praised, Adonai our God, ruler over time and space, our Fathermother, our Creator, Source of our holiness, Sovereign who is good and does good for all. For every single day You have done good, You do good, and may You continue to do good for us. May no goodness ever be lacking from us, from all Israel, and from all the human race.

CONCLUDING PRAYERS

May the Compassionate One send bountiful blessings to this place where we are gathered, and upon this table on which we have eaten.

May the Compassionate One bless all who are gathered here this night.

[On Friday Night Add:]

[May the Compassionate One bestow on us a day of total Sabbath, filled with the restfulness of the life to come.]

(On the First Two Nights Add:)

(May the Compassionate One bestow on us a day that is a complete festival of goodness.)

May the Compassionate One let us merit seeing the days of the Messiah and the life of the World to Come.

עֹשֶׂה שָׁלוֹם בִּמְרוֹמָיו הוּא יַעֲשֶׂה שָׁלוֹם עָלֵינוּ וְעַל־כָּל־יִשְׂרָאֵל וְאִמְרוּ אָמֵן:

O-seh sha-lom bim-ro-mav hu ya-a-seh sha-lom a-lei-nu ve-al kol Yis-ra-el, ve-im-ru a-men.

May the One who makes peace in the high places make peace over us, over all Israel, and over all the world. Amen.

יְיָ עֹז לְעַמּוֹ יִתֵּן יְיָ יְבָרֵךְ אֶת־עַמּוֹ בַשָּׁלוֹם:

A-do-nai oz le-a-mo yi-ten, A-do-nai ye-va-rech et a-mo va-sha-lom.

Adonai, You give strength to your people. May You ever bless Your people with peace.

THE THIRD CUP: Redemption

(A cup of wine may accompany Birkat Ha-Mazon at any meal, but at the Seder it is required, transformed into the Third Cup, the cup for Ve-ga-al-ti, "And I will redeem you with an outstretched arm and great judgments" [Exodus 6:6]. Raise your cups and celebrate with the following words:)

בָּרוּךְ אַתָּה יְיָ אֱלֹהֵינוּ מֶלֶךְ הָעוֹלָם. בּוֹרֵא פְּרִי הַגָּפֶן:

Ba-ruch a-ta A-do-nai E-lo-hei-nu me-lech ha-o-lam, bo-rei pe-ri ha-ga-fen.

Praised are You, Adonai our God, Monarch over time and space, Creator of this fruit of the vine.

DIRECTIONS: Drink from the Third Cup, *Ve-ga-al-ti*, "I will redeem you," while reclining to the left, tasting the holy joy of freedom.

* * * * *

THE CUP OF ELIJAH AND THE OPEN DOOR

(The readings after the meal help us move from the redemption of Mitzrayim to the promise that event holds for the redemption still to come.)

DIRECTIONS: Wine is poured for the Fourth Cup, or this may be delayed until the resumption of Hallel on page 100. The leader also pours wine into the cup designated for Elijah, or, following the custom of Rabbi Naftali of Ropschitz, the Elijah's Cup may be passed around the table. If this is done, all participants should be encouraged to fill this vessel of messianic hope with their own hopes, and with wine from their own cups. The redemption that is to come will be shaped from all our efforts, and all our prayers.

The door is now opened for Elijah, by a child or an adult.

Reflections

(The one who opens the door, or other guests, may say:)

This door could be the Temple door, opened in Jerusalem on the Seder night to receive those who came on foot from all around the country to appear in the place where God could be most intimately encountered.

This door could be the door of every synagogue, opened throughout the ages to demonstrate Jewish innocence before the slanderers who spread rumors of terrible things Jews did behind closed portals on the Seder night.

This door could be the door of every Jewish home, opened before hostile neighbors to show that the Seder celebration was meant to harm none, but to promise justice for the oppressed—and retribution for the oppressors.

This door has also been opened by our oppressors themselves: by the Spanish Inquisition, taking our people out to false trials and executions; by the SS troops of Hitler, dragging our people from their hiding places or their dining tables; by the secret police of the Soviet KGB, hustling our people off to torture in prison or to the Siberian wastes.

But doors have two sides. We spend some moments now recalling how this door has been opened to throw us into the terrifying night of suffering, but let us also recall how it has been opened to rescue us from that night and hold aloft the hope of suffering's end.

May God punish those who have thrown innocents into the void; may God protect those who have saved them.

SHE-FOCH CHA-MAT-CHA

שְׁפֹךְ חֲמָתְךָ אֶל־הַגּוֹיִם אֲשֶׁר לֹא־יְדָעוּךָ וְעַל־מַמְלָכוֹת
אֲשֶׁר בְּשִׁמְךָ לֹא קָרָאוּ: כִּי אָכַל אֶת־יַעֲקֹב וְאֶת־נָוֵהוּ
הֵשַׁמּוּ: שְׁפָךְ־עֲלֵיהֶם זַעְמֶךָ וַחֲרוֹן אַפְּךָ יַשִּׂיגֵם: תִּרְדֹּף
בְּאַף וְתַשְׁמִידֵם מִתַּחַת שְׁמֵי יְיָ:

She-foch cha-mat-cha el ha-go-yim a-sher lo ye-da-u-cha, ve-al mam-le-chot a-sher be-shim-cha lo ka-ra-u. Ki a-chal et Ya-a-kov ve-et na-ve-hu he-sha-mu. She-foch a-lei-hem za-me-cha va-cha-ron ap-cha ya-si-gem. Tir-dof be-af ve-tash-mi-dem mi-ta-chat she-mei A-do-nai.

Pour out Your fury on those peoples that do not know You,
And over realms which do not even call You by Your proper Name;
For such nations have eaten Jacob alive,
Wiping out the places where we peaceably lived,
Pour out Your wrath upon them, let Your burning anger overtake them,
Pursue them with anger, wipe them out from under the heavens of God.
(Psalms 79:6–7, 69:25; Lamentations 3:66)

When People Know Your Proper Name:

Reflections On Opening Doors

(One or more of the following selections may be used. At the conclusion of the reading, turn to page 99 for reflections on Elijah and the closing of the door.)

And then people used to hide themselves. In those days, during 1939, 1940, and part of 1941, people would be seized for forced labor almost every day—so the men hid out in the shops, in cubbies, cellars, garrets. My family used to hide out in a subroom in an old house, on the third floor. Entry was through a trap door in the floor which someone used to cover with a rug and a table on top of it.

The most important problem in any hideout is masking the entry. On the other side of one walled-up room, tiles were pasted into a frame, and the whole thing was pushed aside when people wanted to enter the hideout. In another place, the entry was through a bathroom, in a third through a bakery oven.

Communication with the outside world is another basic problem. Arrangements are made in advance with a Christian, who looks after the needs of the Jews in the hideout on the days when they go into hiding.

*　*　*　*　*

(After the Nazis had conquered France, a small Protestant village in southern France called Le Chambon, under its dedicated pastor André Trocmé and his wife Magda, developed a system for hiding and protecting Jews within its members' homes.)

In physics the analysis of forces is useful. For instance, one may break down the various forces at work upon a door and upon the frame in which it is hung in order to hang the door well. But analysis is not all there is. There is another aspect to the full reality of this movement of the well-hung, opening door. There is the *experience*, so ordinary, perhaps, to be unnoticed, of simply opening and closing a door.

If you are interested in understanding what happened in Le Chambon in a way similar to the way the Chambon residents themselves looked at what they did, then their actions become rather easy to understand. They become as easy to understand as Magda Trocmé rushing in her frenetic way from the kitchen to the presbytery door, turning the doorknob, and opening the door for a refugee with, "Naturally, come in, and come in."

If we would understand the goodness that happened in Le Chambon, we must see how easy it was for them to refuse to give up their consciences, to refuse to participate in hatred, betrayal, and murder, and to help the desperate adults and the terrified children who knocked on their doors in Le Chambon. Goodness is the simplest thing in the world, and the most complex, like opening a door.

*　*　*　*　*

(In June 1964, seventeen members of the Central Conference of American Rabbis responded to Dr. Martin Luther King's urgent request to join him in a demonstration against segregation in St. Augustine, Florida, the oldest city in the United States. Imprisoned after the demonstration, they wrote the following letter, excerpted here, sitting on the floor behind the locked doors of their cell.)

Why We Went

We came because we realized that injustice in St. Augustine, as anywhere else, diminishes the humanity of each of us. We came to St. Augustine mainly because we could not stay away. We could not pass by the opportunity to achieve a moral goal by moral means—a rare modern privilege—which has been the glory of the non-violent struggle for civil rights.

We came because we could not stand silently by our brother's blood. We had done that too many times before. We came in the hope that the God of us all would accept our small involvement as partial atonement for the many things we wish we had done before and often.

We came as Jews who remember the millions of faceless people who stood quietly, watching the smoke rise from Hitler's crematoria. We came because we know that second only to silence, the greatest danger to humanity is loss of faith in humanity's capacity to act.

We shall not soon forget the stirring and heartfelt excitement with which the Black community greeted us with full-throated hymns and hallelujahs, which pulsated and resounded through the church; nor the bond of affectionate solidarity which joined us hand in hand during our marches through town; nor the common purpose which transcended our fears as well as the boundaries of race, geography, and circumstance. We hope we have strengthened the morale of St. Augustine Blacks as they strive to claim their dignity; we know they have strengthened ours.

These words were first written at 3:00 a.m. in the sweltering heat of a sleepless night, by the light of the one naked bulb hanging in the corridor outside our small cell. At daybreak we revised the contents of the letter and prayed together for a new dawn of justice and mercy for all the children of God.

Baruch ata Adonai matir asurim. Blessed art Thou, O God, who opens the door for the captives.

* * * * *

We have opened the door in the hope that Elijah the Prophet might enter and announce that the Messiah, a descendant of King David, is about to arrive and usher in the time of redemption for all humanity. But the line of David has become commingled with all other families, and we no longer know who are his heirs. It is therefore possible that anyone—anyone seated around this table—might be his heir. God might choose any one of us to help redeem the world.

If Elijah comes tonight, he will announce who has been found worthy to take that role. If he does not come—or if we are not sure whether he has come—we must close the door, against anyone who tells us that our society, our people, our world, is messianic, ideal, the best possible. If we cannot see Elijah enter, it means God has asked each of us here tonight to help realize the world for which all people yearn.

Song: Eliyahu Ha-Navi

אֵלִיָהוּ הַנָּבִיא. אֵלִיָהוּ הַתִּשְׁבִּי. אֵלִיָהוּ. אֵלִיָהוּ. אֵלִיָהוּ
הַגִּלְעָדִי. בִּמְהֵרָה בְיָמֵינוּ יָבֹא אֵלֵינוּ עִם מָשִׁיחַ בֶּן דָּוִד:

Ei-li-ya-hu ha-na-vi, Ei-li-ya-hu ha-Tish-bi, Ei-li-ya-hu, Ei-li-ya-hu, Ei-li-ya-hu ha-Gi-la-di. Bim-hei-ra ve-ya-mei-nu, ya-vo ei-lei-nu, im ma-shi-ach ben Da-vid.

Elijah the Prophet, Elijah the Tishbite, Elijah of Gilead: may he soon come and bring the Messiah.

(If Elijah seems not to come, all say:)

We have failed the test of the open door—yet in our failure lies our hope as human beings. We have opened the door and looked only into darkness—but the darkness calls each one of us to help to bring the light.

DIRECTIONS: The door is closed.

(Other songs that might be sung here, reflecting shared human dreams of redemption and peace, are "The Hammer Song," "Follow the Drinking Gourd," "Lo Yissa Goy," "Down by the Riverside," "We Shall Overcome," or "Ally, Ally Oxen Free," beginning on p. 145)

הַלֵּל

HALLEL

And Now with Praise

DIRECTIONS: In the spirit of the hope for redemption suggested by the open door, we conclude the psalms of Hallel, of praise, begun before the meal. Some people prefer to pour the Fourth Cup of wine at this point. Continue to offer up these psalms with joy:

Psalm 115:1–11

לֹא לָנוּ יְיָ לֹא לָנוּ כִּי לְשִׁמְךָ תֵּן כָּבוֹד עַל־חַסְדְּךָ עַל־
אֲמִתֶּךָ: לָמָּה יֹאמְרוּ הַגּוֹיִם אַיֵּה־נָא אֱלֹהֵיהֶם: וֵאלֹהֵינוּ
בַשָּׁמָיִם כֹּל אֲשֶׁר־חָפֵץ עָשָׂה: עֲצַבֵּיהֶם כֶּסֶף וְזָהָב
מַעֲשֵׂה יְדֵי אָדָם: פֶּה־לָהֶם וְלֹא יְדַבֵּרוּ עֵינַיִם לָהֶם וְלֹא
יִרְאוּ: אָזְנַיִם לָהֶם וְלֹא יִשְׁמָעוּ אַף לָהֶם וְלֹא יְרִיחוּן:
יְדֵיהֶם וְלֹא יְמִישׁוּן רַגְלֵיהֶם וְלֹא יְהַלֵּכוּ לֹא־יֶהְגּוּ
בִּגְרוֹנָם: כְּמוֹהֶם יִהְיוּ עֹשֵׂיהֶם כֹּל אֲשֶׁר־בֹּטֵחַ בָּהֶם:
יִשְׂרָאֵל בְּטַח בַּיְיָ עֶזְרָם וּמָגִנָּם הוּא: בֵּית אַהֲרֹן בִּטְחוּ בַיְיָ
עֶזְרָם וּמָגִנָּם הוּא: יִרְאֵי יְיָ בִּטְחוּ בַיְיָ עֶזְרָם וּמָגִנָּם הוּא:

Lo la-nu A-do-nai, lo la-nu, ki le-shim-cha ten ka-vod al chas-de-cha, al a-mi-te-cha; la-ma yo-me-ru ha-go-yim: a-yei-na e-lo-hei-hem. Vei-lo-hei-nu va-sha-ma-yim, kol a-sher cha-fetz a-sah. A-tza-bei-hem ke-sef ve-za-hav ma-a-sei ye-dei a-dam. Peh la-hem ve-lo ye-da-bei-ru, ei-na-yim la-hem ve-lo yir-u, oz-na-yim la-hem ve-lo yish-ma-u, af la-hem ve-lo ye-ri-chun. Ye-dei-hem ve-lo ye-mi-shun, rag-lei-hem ve-lo ye-ha-lei-chu, lo ye-he-gu bi-gro-nam. Ke-mo-hem yi-he-yu o-sei-hem, kol a-sher bo-tei-ach ba-hem. Yis-ra-el be-tach vA-do-nai, ez-ram u-ma-gi-nam hu. Beit A-ha-ron bit-chu vA-do-nai, ez-ram u-ma-gi-nam hu. Yir-ei A-do-nai, bit-chu vA-do-nai, ez-ram u-ma-gi-nam hu.

Not to us who sit here,
Mere beneficiaries of Your redemption,
Not to us,
But to Your Name grant honor,
For Your love and Your truth.

Why do the peoples say, "Where is your God now?"
Our God is in the heavens! Whatever You will, You do.
Their idols are silver and gold, handmade,
With mouths that do not speak
Eyes that do not see
Ears that do not hear
A nose that does not smell
Hands that do not feel
Feet that do not move.
They make no sound in their throats.
Just like them are those who make them
And those who trust in them.

O Israel, trust in the Eternal, our help and our shield!
O House of Aaron, trust in the Eternal, your help and your
    shield!
O you who revere the Eternal, trust in the Eternal, your help
    and your shield!

Psalm 115:12–18

יְיָ זְכָרָנוּ יְבָרֵךְ יְבָרֵךְ אֶת־בֵּית יִשְׂרָאֵל יְבָרֵךְ אֶת־בֵּית
אַהֲרֹן: יְבָרֵךְ יִרְאֵי יְיָ הַקְּטַנִּים עִם־הַגְּדֹלִים: יֹסֵף יְיָ
עֲלֵיכֶם עֲלֵיכֶם וְעַל־בְּנֵיכֶם: בְּרוּכִים אַתֶּם לַיְיָ עֹשֵׂה
שָׁמַיִם וָאָרֶץ: הַשָּׁמַיִם שָׁמַיִם לַיְיָ וְהָאָרֶץ נָתַן לִבְנֵי־אָדָם:
לֹא הַמֵּתִים יְהַלְלוּ־יָהּ וְלֹא כָּל־יֹרְדֵי דוּמָה: וַאֲנַחְנוּ
נְבָרֵךְ יָהּ מֵעַתָּה וְעַד־עוֹלָם הַלְלוּיָהּ:

A-do-nai ze-cha-ra-nu ye-va-rech, ye-va-rech et beit
Yis-ra-el, ye-va-rech et beit A-ha-ron. Ye-va-rech yir-ei
A-do-nai ha-ke-ta-nim im ha-ge-do-lim. Yo-sef A-do-nai
a-lei-chem, a-lei-chem ve-al be-nei-chem. Be-ru-chim
a-tem lA-do-nai o-sei sha-ma-yim va-a-retz. Ha-sha-

ma-yim sha-ma-yim lA-do-nai ve-ha-a-retz na-tan liv-
nei a-dam, lo ha-mei-tim ye-ha-le-lu-Ya ve-lo kol yor-dei
du-mah, va-a-nach-nu ne-va-rech Ya me-a-ta ve-ad
o-lam. Ha-le-lu-Ya!

Adonai, You have brought us into Your presence,
Remembering us for the blessing of a fruitful life.
May You bless the house of Israel,
May You bless the house of Aaron,
May You bless those who revere You.

May Adonai cause you to increase,
You and your children with you.
May you be blessed by the Source of blessing,
The maker of heaven and earth.
The heavens are the heavens of God,
But the earth was given over to the children of Adam and
    Eve,
To us.

The dead cannot sing Hallelu-Ya,
Nor can those who go silently to the grave;
But so long as we live,
Let us praise God,
Let everything we do praise God,
From this moment till eternity,
In this place and in every place:
Praise be to Ya!
Hallelu-Ya!

Psalm 116:1–11

אָהַבְתִּי כִּי־יִשְׁמַע יְיָ אֶת־קוֹלִי תַּחֲנוּנָי: כִּי־הִטָּה אָזְנוֹ לִי
וּבְיָמַי אֶקְרָא: אֲפָפוּנִי חֶבְלֵי־מָוֶת וּמְצָרֵי שְׁאוֹל מְצָאוּנִי
צָרָה וְיָגוֹן אֶמְצָא: וּבְשֵׁם יְיָ אֶקְרָא אָנָּה יְיָ מַלְּטָה נַפְשִׁי:
חַנּוּן יְיָ וְצַדִּיק וֵאלֹהֵינוּ מְרַחֵם: שֹׁמֵר פְּתָאיִם יְיָ דַּלֹּתִי
וְלִי יְהוֹשִׁיעַ: שׁוּבִי נַפְשִׁי לִמְנוּחָיְכִי כִּי־יְיָ גָּמַל עָלָיְכִי: כִּי
חִלַּצְתָּ נַפְשִׁי מִמָּוֶת אֶת־עֵינִי מִן־דִּמְעָה אֶת־רַגְלִי מִדֶּחִי:
אֶתְהַלֵּךְ לִפְנֵי יְיָ בְּאַרְצוֹת הַחַיִּים: הֶאֱמַנְתִּי כִּי אֲדַבֵּר אֲנִי
עָנִיתִי מְאֹד: אֲנִי אָמַרְתִּי בְחָפְזִי כָּל־הָאָדָם כֹּזֵב:

I am filled with love
For God is listening to my voice,
My plea.

I am filled with love,
For Your ear has turned toward me,
And so I shall continue to call out to You
All my days:

> The bonds of death have tied me up,
> The Mitzrayim of the grave have found me
> And I have found pain and sorrow.
> And so I call out Your name, Adonai—
> Adonai, rescue my soul!

Adonai is gracious and just,
Our God is filled with love,
Adonai watches over simple people.
How low I had fallen, and God rescued me!

Come home, O my soul, to thy resting place,
For Adonai has acted generously toward thee.
You have delivered my soul from death,
My eye from tears, my foot from stumbling,
That I might walk in the presence of God in lands full of life.

Because of my faith
I can speak to You of my suffering:
I am in such pain!
I can speak to You of my alarm:
Everyone is lying!

Psalm 116:12–19

מָה־אָשִׁיב לַיְיָ כָּל־תַּגְמוּלֹהִי עָלָי: כּוֹס־יְשׁוּעוֹת אֶשָּׂא
וּבְשֵׁם יְיָ אֶקְרָא: נְדָרַי לַיְיָ אֲשַׁלֵּם נֶגְדָה־נָּא לְכָל־עַמּוֹ:
יָקָר בְּעֵינֵי יְיָ הַמָּוְתָה לַחֲסִידָיו: אָנָּה יְיָ כִּי־אֲנִי עַבְדֶּךָ אֲנִי
עַבְדְּךָ בֶּן־אֲמָתֶךָ פִּתַּחְתָּ לְמוֹסֵרָי: לְךָ אֶזְבַּח זֶבַח תּוֹדָה
וּבְשֵׁם יְיָ אֶקְרָא: נְדָרַי לַיְיָ אֲשַׁלֵּם נֶגְדָה־נָּא לְכָל־עַמּוֹ:
בְּחַצְרוֹת בֵּית יְיָ בְּתוֹכֵכִי יְרוּשָׁלָיִם הַלְלוּיָהּ:

Somehow, You returned to me an answer.
What can I return to Adonai
For all Your favors to me?
I shall lift up this cup of righteous victory
And call out Your Name: *Adonai!*
In the presence of all the people
I shall make good what I have vowed.
The more kindly I live my life
The more precious will be my death
In the eyes of God.

Adonai, I am Your servant,
My mother has been Your servant,
You have unlocked the shackles
Imposed by those who would have me serve them.

I will offer You a gift that shows my thankfulness,
I shall call out Your Name: *Adonai!*
I shall make good what I have vowed
In the presence of all the people,
In the courts of the House of God,
In thine inmost parts, O Jerusalem.
Everyone sing praise to Ya:
Hallelu-Ya!

Psalm 117

הַלְלוּ אֶת־יְיָ כָּל־גּוֹיִם שַׁבְּחוּהוּ כָּל־הָאֻמִּים: כִּי גָבַר
עָלֵינוּ חַסְדּוֹ וֶאֱמֶת־יְיָ לְעוֹלָם הַלְלוּיָהּ:

Ha-le-lu et A-do-nai, kol go-yim
Sha-be-chu-hu kol ha-u-mim
Ki ga-var a-lei-nu chas-do
Ve-e-met A-do-nai le-o-lam,
Ha-le-lu-Ya!

Sing hallel to Adonai, all peoples!
Praise God, all nations!
For God's love empowers us,
God's truth immortalizes us,
Hallelu-Ya!

Psalm 118:1–4

הוֹדוּ לַיָי כִּי־טוֹב כִּי לְעוֹלָם חַסְדּוֹ:
יֹאמַר־נָא יִשְׂרָאֵל כִּי לְעוֹלָם חַסְדּוֹ:
יֹאמְרוּ־נָא בֵית־אַהֲרֹן כִּי לְעוֹלָם חַסְדּוֹ:
יֹאמְרוּ־נָא יִרְאֵי יְיָ כִּי לְעוֹלָם חַסְדּוֹ:

Ho-du lA-do-nai ki tov, ki le-o-lam chas-do,
Yo-mar na Yis-ra-el ki le-o-lam chas-do,
Yom-ru na veit A-ha-ron ki le-o-lam chas-do,
Yom-ru na yir-ei A-do-nai ki le-o-lam chas-do.

Give thanks to Adonai: how good You are! Your love is
    eternal!
Let Israel say as one: how good You are! Your love is eternal!
Let the house of Aaron say, everyone: how good You are!
    Your love is eternal!
Let those who revere Adonai say, everyone: how good You
    are! Your love is eternal!

Psalm 118:5–20

מִן־הַמֵּצַר קָרָאתִי יָּה עָנָנִי בַמֶּרְחַב יָה: יְיָ לִי לֹא אִירָא
מַה־יַּעֲשֶׂה לִי אָדָם: יְיָ לִי בְּעֹזְרָי וַאֲנִי אֶרְאֶה בְשֹׂנְאָי:
טוֹב לַחֲסוֹת בַּיָי מִבְּטֹחַ בָּאָדָם: טוֹב לַחֲסוֹת בַּיָי מִבְּטֹחַ
בִּנְדִיבִים: כָּל־גּוֹיִם סְבָבוּנִי בְּשֵׁם יְיָ כִּי אֲמִילַם: סַבּוּנִי
גַם־סְבָבוּנִי בְּשֵׁם יְיָ כִּי אֲמִילַם: סַבּוּנִי כִדְבֹרִים דֹּעֲכוּ
כְּאֵשׁ קוֹצִים בְּשֵׁם יְיָ כִּי אֲמִילַם: דָּחֹה דְחִיתַנִי לִנְפֹּל וַיְיָ
עֲזָרָנִי: עָזִּי וְזִמְרָת יָה וַיְהִי־לִי לִישׁוּעָה: קוֹל רִנָּה
וִישׁוּעָה בְּאָהֳלֵי צַדִּיקִים יְמִין יְיָ עֹשָׂה חָיִל: יְמִין יְיָ
רוֹמֵמָה יְמִין יְיָ עֹשָׂה חָיִל: לֹא־אָמוּת כִּי־אֶחְיֶה וַאֲסַפֵּר
מַעֲשֵׂי יָהּ: יַסֹּר יִסְּרַנִי יָּהּ וְלַמָּוֶת לֹא נְתָנָנִי: פִּתְחוּ־לִי
שַׁעֲרֵי־צֶדֶק אָבֹא־בָם אוֹדֶה יָהּ: זֶה־הַשַּׁעַר לַיָי צַדִּיקִים
יָבֹאוּ בוֹ:

Min ha-mei-tzar ka-ra-ti Ya, a-na-ni va-mer-chav Ya. Adonai li lo i-ra, ma ya-a-seh li a-dam? A-do-nai li be-oz-rai va-a-ni er-eh ve-son-ai. Tov la-cha-sot bA-do-nai mi-be-to-ach ba-a-dam; tov la-cha-sot bA-do-nai mi-be-to-ach bi-ne-di-vim. Kol go-yim se-va-vu-ni be-shem A-do-nai ki a-mi-lam, sa-bu-ni gam se-va-vu-ni, be-shem A-do-nai ki a-mi-lam. Sa-bu-ni chi-de-vo-rim, do-a-chu ke-esh ko-tzim, be-shem A-do-nai ki a-mi-lam. Da-cho de-chi-ta-ni lin-pol vA-do-nai a-za-ra-ni, o-zi ve-zim-rat Ya, va-ye-hi li li-shu-a. Kol ri-na vi-shu-a be-o-ho-lei tza-di-kim ye-min A-do-nai o-sa cha-yil ye-min A-do-nai ro-mei-ma ye-min A-do-nai o-sa cha-yil lo a-mut ki ech-yeh va-a-sa-per ma-a-sei Ya. Ya-sor yis-ra-ni Ya ve-la-ma-vet lo ne-ta-na-ni. Pit-chu li sha-a-rei tze-dek a-vo vam o-deh Ya. Zeh ha-sha-ar lA-do-nai tza-di-kim ya-vo-u vo.

From Mitzrayim, the narrows of my life,
I cried out: You!
And You responded.

How much room I have!
I have Adonai, I need not fear,
What can any person do to me?
I have Adonai, my helper,
So I can stare down my enemies.
It is good to trust in God
More than in human beings,
Good to trust in God
More than in the noblest human beings.

Though all the peoples encircle me,
In the name of God I will turn aside their power
Into the service of the covenant.
They may encircle me; let them encircle me on every side!
In the name of God I will turn aside their power
Into the service of the covenant.
Though they encircle me like bees
They will dry up like thorns in a fire.
In the name of God I will turn aside their power
Into the service of the covenant.

You made me stumble and fall,
But God assisted me.

As we cried out at the Reed Sea:
My strength and my song is You,
You have brought me a righteous victory!

Hear the victorious singing in the homes of righteous
    people:
    Mighty acts come from the right hand of God!
    High and exalted is the right hand of God!
    Mighty acts come from the right hand of God!

I shall not die!
I shall live instead, I shall tell tales
About the acts of You,
Who though leaving me sorely chastened
Has not given me over to death.
So open the gates of justice for me,
I'm coming through them to give thanks to You.
This is the gate of God,
Those judged innocent will come through it.

Psalm 118:21–24

DIRECTIONS: Offer each line twice.

אוֹדְךָ כִּי עֲנִיתָנִי וַתְּהִי־לִי לִישׁוּעָה:
אֶבֶן מָאֲסוּ הַבּוֹנִים הָיְתָה לְרֹאשׁ פִּנָּה:
מֵאֵת יְיָ הָיְתָה זֹּאת הִיא נִפְלָאת בְּעֵינֵינוּ:
זֶה־הַיּוֹם עָשָׂה יְיָ נָגִילָה וְנִשְׂמְחָה בוֹ:

O-de-cha ki a-ni-ta-ni, va-te-hi li li-shu-a.
E-ven ma-a-su ha-bo-nim ha-ye-ta le-rosh pi-na.
Me-et A-do-nai ha-ye-ta zot, hi nif-lat be-ei-nei-nu.
Zeh ha-yom a-sa A-do-nai, na-gi-la ve-nis-me-cha vo.

Thank You for responding to me, for giving me this victory:
A stone spurned by the builders now holds up the gate!
The work of God was this, astonishing to see,
This is the day Adonai has made; now let us rejoice and be
    jubilant!

Psalm 118:25

A-na A-do-nai ho-shi-a na   אָנָּא יְיָ הוֹשִׁיעָה נָּא.

A-na A-do-nai ho-shi-a na   אָנָּא יְיָ הוֹשִׁיעָה נָּא׃

A-na A-do-nai hatz-li-cha na   אָנָּא יְיָ הַצְלִיחָה נָא.

A-na A-do-nai hatz-li-cha na!   אָנָּא יְיָ הַצְלִיחָה נָא׃

O Adonai, over enemies and adversity, over sickness and
    despair,
Help us achieve a righteous victory!
O Adonai, help us to flourish!
O Adonai, help us to thrive!

Psalm 118:26–29

DIRECTIONS: Offer each line twice.

בָּרוּךְ הַבָּא בְּשֵׁם יְיָ בֵּרַכְנוּכֶם מִבֵּית יְיָ׃

אֵל יְיָ וַיָּאֶר לָנוּ אִסְרוּ־חַג בַּעֲבֹתִים עַד־קַרְנוֹת הַמִּזְבֵּחַ׃

אֵלִי אַתָּה וְאוֹדֶךָּ אֱלֹהַי אֲרוֹמְמֶךָּ׃

הוֹדוּ לַייָ כִּי־טוֹב כִּי לְעוֹלָם חַסְדּוֹ׃

Ba-ruch ha-ba be-shem A-do-nai, be-rach-nu-chem mi-
    beit A-do-nai.
El A-do-nai va-ya-er la-nu, is-ru chag ba-a-vo-tim ad
    kar-not ha-miz-bei-ach.
Ei-li a-ta ve-o-de-ka, E-lo-hai a-ro-me-me-ka.
Ho-du lA-do-nai ki tov, ki le-o-lam chas-do.

DIRECTIONS: Like the Levitical choirs in the Temple, half the company
might proclaim each line, with the other half repeating it in response.

May everyone who has come to this place be blessed in the
    Name of God!
We welcome you with a blessing from the house of God!
Adonai is God, giving us light,
Tie up the festival offering with cords, bring it up to the
    altar!
You are my God and I give You thanks,
My just God and I will raise Your Name high!
Give thanks to God: how good You are! Your love is eternal!

יְהַלְלוּךְ יְיָ אֱלֹהֵינוּ כָּל־מַעֲשֶׂיךָ. וַחֲסִידֶיךָ צַדִּיקִים עוֹשֵׂי
רְצוֹנֶךָ. וְכָל־עַמְּךָ בֵּית־יִשְׂרָאֵל בְּרִנָּה יוֹדוּ וִיבָרְכוּ
וִישַׁבְּחוּ וִיפָאֲרוּ וִירוֹמְמוּ וְיַעֲרִיצוּ וְיַקְדִּישׁוּ וְיַמְלִיכוּ
אֶת־שִׁמְךָ מַלְכֵּנוּ: כִּי לְךָ טוֹב לְהוֹדוֹת. וּלְשִׁמְךָ נָאֶה
לְזַמֵּר. כִּי מֵעוֹלָם וְעַד־עוֹלָם אַתָּה אֵל:

Ye-ha-le-lu-cha A-do-nai E-lo-hei-nu kol ma-a-se-cha,
va-cha-si-de-cha tza-di-kim o-sei re-tzo-ne-cha. Ve-chol
am-cha beit Yis-ra-el be-ri-na yo-du vi-va-re-chu vi-sha-
be-chu vi-fa-a-ru vi-ro-me-mu ve-ya-a-ri-tzu ve-yak-
di-shu ve-yam-li-chu et shim-cha mal-kei-nu. Ki le-cha
tov le-ho-dot u-le-shim-cha na-eh le-za-mer. Ki me-o-
lam ve-ad o-lam a-ta El.

May all Your works sing hallel to You, Adonai our God,
May all Your pious ones sing, all the righteous, as they do
    Your will.
May all Your people the house of Israel
With joy say thanks
And bless and praise, laud, exalt, and exult in Your Name,
Reveal Your holiness, Your rule over their lives,
For it is good to say thanks to You,
Pleasant to sing to Your Name.
For from this world into the next,
God
Is You.

THE FIFTH CUP: First Part

(Those who wish to follow the rite of the great Maharal of Prague,
Rabbi Judah Loewe, and drink a fifth cup of wine to com-
memorate the fifth promise, "And I shall bring you into the land"
(Exodus 6:8), a promise suggesting the messianic fulfillment,
should drink the fourth cup here, continuing on the top of page
110.

If you do not wish to follow the rite of the Fifth Cup, continue
with "The Great Hallel," page 110.)

Reflections

The Fourth Cup celebrates *Ve-la-kach-ti*, "I will take you to Me for a people and I will become God for you" (Exodus 6:7). In this cup we may see expressed the hope for spiritual redemption, for the fulfillment of our longing to be close to God. The more we act like God's people, this fourth promise suggests, the more we can experience the Eternal One becoming God for each of us.

Let us raise our cups and celebrate that promise with the following words:

בָּרוּךְ אַתָּה יְיָ אֱלֹהֵינוּ מֶלֶךְ הָעוֹלָם. בּוֹרֵא פְּרִי הַגָּפֶן.

Ba-ruch a-ta A-do-nai E-lo-hei-nu me-lech ha-o-lam, bo-rei pe-ri ha-ga-fen.

Praised are You, Adonai our God, Monarch over time and space, Creator of this fruit of the vine.

DIRECTIONS: Drink from the Fourth Cup, *Ve-la-kach-ti*, "I will take you," while reclining to the left, tasting the holy joy of God's presence.

The Fifth Cup is now poured, or the Cup of Elijah may be used, and the Great Hallel is offered, below.

THE GREAT HALLEL (Psalm 136)

הוֹדוּ לַיְיָ כִּי־טוֹב כִּי לְעוֹלָם חַסְדּוֹ:

הוֹדוּ לֵאלֹהֵי הָאֱלֹהִים כִּי לְעוֹלָם חַסְדּוֹ:

הוֹדוּ לַאֲדֹנֵי הָאֲדֹנִים כִּי לְעוֹלָם חַסְדּוֹ:

לְעֹשֵׂה נִפְלָאוֹת גְּדֹלוֹת לְבַדּוֹ כִּי לְעוֹלָם חַסְדּוֹ:

לְעֹשֵׂה הַשָּׁמַיִם בִּתְבוּנָה כִּי לְעוֹלָם חַסְדּוֹ:

לְרוֹקַע הָאָרֶץ עַל־הַמָּיִם כִּי לְעוֹלָם חַסְדּוֹ:

לְעֹשֵׂה אוֹרִים גְּדֹלִים כִּי לְעוֹלָם חַסְדּוֹ:

אֶת־הַשֶּׁמֶשׁ לְמֶמְשֶׁלֶת בַּיּוֹם כִּי לְעוֹלָם חַסְדּוֹ:

אֶת־הַיָּרֵחַ וְכוֹכָבִים לְמֶמְשְׁלוֹת בַּלָּיְלָה כִּי לְעוֹלָם חַסְדּוֹ:

לְמַכֵּה מִצְרַיִם בִּבְכוֹרֵיהֶם כִּי לְעוֹלָם חַסְדּוֹ:

וַיּוֹצֵא יִשְׂרָאֵל מִתּוֹכָם כִּי לְעוֹלָם חַסְדּוֹ:

בְּיָד חֲזָקָה וּבִזְרוֹעַ נְטוּיָה כִּי לְעוֹלָם חַסְדּוֹ:
לְגֹזֵר יַם־סוּף לִגְזָרִים כִּי לְעוֹלָם חַסְדּוֹ:
וְהֶעֱבִיר יִשְׂרָאֵל בְּתוֹכוֹ כִּי לְעוֹלָם חַסְדּוֹ:
וְנִעֵר פַּרְעֹה וְחֵילוֹ בְיַם־סוּף כִּי לְעוֹלָם חַסְדּוֹ:
לְמוֹלִיךְ עַמּוֹ בַּמִּדְבָּר כִּי לְעוֹלָם חַסְדּוֹ:
לְמַכֵּה מְלָכִים גְּדוֹלִים כִּי לְעוֹלָם חַסְדּוֹ:
וַיַּהֲרֹג מְלָכִים אַדִּירִים כִּי לְעוֹלָם חַסְדּוֹ:
לְסִיחוֹן מֶלֶךְ הָאֱמֹרִי כִּי לְעוֹלָם חַסְדּוֹ:
וּלְעוֹג מֶלֶךְ הַבָּשָׁן כִּי לְעוֹלָם חַסְדּוֹ:
וְנָתַן אַרְצָם לְנַחֲלָה כִּי לְעוֹלָם חַסְדּוֹ:
נַחֲלָה לְיִשְׂרָאֵל עַבְדּוֹ כִּי לְעוֹלָם חַסְדּוֹ:
שֶׁבְּשִׁפְלֵנוּ זָכַר לָנוּ כִּי לְעוֹלָם חַסְדּוֹ:
וַיִּפְרְקֵנוּ מִצָּרֵינוּ כִּי לְעוֹלָם חַסְדּוֹ:
נֹתֵן לֶחֶם לְכָל בָּשָׂר כִּי לְעוֹלָם חַסְדּוֹ:
הוֹדוּ לְאֵל הַשָּׁמָיִם כִּי לְעוֹלָם חַסְדּוֹ:

DIRECTIONS: If this psalm is to be read in English, each person around the table might read a verse in turn, with the whole company responding each time with, "Your love is eternal!"

Give thanks to Adonai, how good You are! Your love is eternal!
Give thanks to the God of all the gods, Your love is eternal!
Give thanks to the power over all earthly powers, Your love is eternal!
To the One who all alone makes great wonders: Your love is eternal!
To the One who makes the heavens through wisdom: Your love is eternal!
To the One who spreads the earth over the waters: Your love is eternal!
To the One who makes great lights: Your love is eternal!
Who makes the sun for dominion by day: Your love is eternal!

Who makes the moon and stars for dominion by night: Your love is eternal!

To the smiter of Mitzrayim through the firstborn: Your love is eternal!

Who brought Israel out from their midst: Your love is eternal!

With a mighty hand and an outstretched arm: Your love is eternal!

To the Divider of the Reed Sea into two parts: Your love is eternal!

Who caused Israel to pass through its midst: Your love is eternal!

And threw Pharaoh and his army into the Reed Sea: Your love is eternal!

To become a leader of Your people in the wilderness: Your love is eternal!

To the smiter of mighty monarchs: Your love is eternal!

Who slew powerful monarchs: Your love is eternal!

Sichon, the Amorite monarch: Your love is eternal!

And Og, the monarch of Bashan: Your love is eternal!

And gave over their land as an inheritance: Your love is eternal!

An inheritance to Israel the servant of God: Your love is eternal!

Who was present to us in our humbled state: Your love is eternal!

And snatched us away from our oppressors: Your love is eternal!

Giving food to all flesh: Your love is eternal!

Give thanks to the God of heaven, for Your love is eternal!

NISHMAT: A Celebration of Our Soul

נִשְׁמַת כָּל־חַי תְּבָרֵךְ אֶת־שִׁמְךָ יְיָ אֱלֹהֵינוּ. וְרוּחַ
כָּל־בָּשָׂר תְּפָאֵר וּתְרוֹמֵם זִכְרְךָ מַלְכֵּנוּ תָּמִיד. מִן־
הָעוֹלָם וְעַד־הָעוֹלָם אַתָּה אֵל. וּמִבַּלְעָדֶיךָ אֵין לָנוּ מֶלֶךְ
גּוֹאֵל וּמוֹשִׁיעַ פּוֹדֶה וּמַצִּיל וּמְפַרְנֵס וּמְרַחֵם בְּכָל־עֵת
צָרָה וְצוּקָה אֵין־לָנוּ מֶלֶךְ אֶלָּא אָתָּה: אֱלֹהֵי הָרִאשׁוֹנִים

וְהָאַחֲרוֹנִים. אֱלוֹהַ כָּל־בְּרִיוֹת אֲדוֹן כָּל־תּוֹלָדוֹת.
הַמְהֻלָּל בְּרֹב הַתִּשְׁבָּחוֹת. הַמְנַהֵג עוֹלָמוֹ בְּחֶסֶד
וּבְרִיּוֹתָיו בְּרַחֲמִים. וַיָי לֹא־יָנוּם וְלֹא־יִישָׁן: הַמְעוֹרֵר
יְשֵׁנִים וְהַמֵּקִיץ נִרְדָּמִים וְהַמֵּשִׂיחַ אִלְּמִים וְהַמַּתִּיר
אֲסוּרִים וְהַסּוֹמֵךְ נוֹפְלִים וְהַזּוֹקֵף כְּפוּפִים. לְךָ לְבַדְּךָ
אֲנַחְנוּ מוֹדִים:

Let the soul of everything alive
Sing praises to Your name!
Let the breath of every creature glorify and praise
The signs of divinity in time,
The traces of holy rule in every place!
In the face of the evils of these years,
The pain and suffering of human life,
Let us feel the touch of forces
    freeing us from bondage,
    winning victories over enemies
    within us and without.

Adonai does not sleep.
Those who lead sleepy lives
God stirs awake,
Those who live without words
God stirs to speak.

אִלּוּ פִינוּ מָלֵא שִׁירָה כַיָּם וּלְשׁוֹנֵנוּ רִנָּה כַּהֲמוֹן גַּלָּיו
וְשִׂפְתוֹתֵינוּ שֶׁבַח כְּמֶרְחֲבֵי רָקִיעַ וְעֵינֵינוּ מְאִירוֹת
כַּשֶּׁמֶשׁ וְכַיָּרֵחַ וְיָדֵינוּ פְרוּשׂוֹת כְּנִשְׁרֵי שָׁמַיִם וְרַגְלֵינוּ
קַלּוֹת כָּאַיָּלוֹת. אֵין אֲנַחְנוּ מַסְפִּיקִים לְהוֹדוֹת לְךָ יְיָ
אֱלֹהֵינוּ וֵאלֹהֵי אֲבוֹתֵינוּ (וְאִמּוֹתֵינוּ) וּלְבָרֵךְ אֶת־שְׁמֶךָ
עַל־אַחַת מֵאָלֶף אֶלֶף אַלְפֵי אֲלָפִים וְרִבֵּי רְבָבוֹת פְּעָמִים
הַטּוֹבוֹת שֶׁעָשִׂיתָ עִם־אֲבוֹתֵינוּ (וְאִמּוֹתֵינוּ) וְעִמָּנוּ.
מִמִּצְרַיִם גְּאַלְתָּנוּ יְיָ אֱלֹהֵינוּ וּמִבֵּית עֲבָדִים פְּדִיתָנוּ.
בְּרָעָב זַנְתָּנוּ וּבְשָׂבָע כִּלְכַּלְתָּנוּ. מֵחֶרֶב הִצַּלְתָּנוּ וּמִדֶּבֶר
מִלַּטְתָּנוּ. וּמֵחֳלָיִם רָעִים וְנֶאֱמָנִים דִּלִּיתָנוּ: עַד־הֵנָּה

עֲזָרוּנוּ רַחֲמֶיךָ. וְלֹא עֲזָבוּנוּ חֲסָדֶיךָ. וְאַל־תִּטְּשֵׁנוּ יְיָ אֱלֹהֵינוּ לָנֶצַח:

If our mouths filled with song like the sea,
If our tongue could roar like the surf,
If our lips billowed praise like a bright day's sky—
Our eyes the sun, or by night the moon—
If our arms could spread like the pinions of eagles
And our legs make us fly over fields like gazelles—
Still would our lips lack words
And our bodies the space
To acknowledge the brilliance even of a handful of world
Pervaded by Adonai,
Or speak a blessing even for the tiniest goodness You have
    done,
God for our fathers, our mothers, and for us.

From Mitzrayim You redeemed us,
From the house of slaves You ransomed us,
In hungry times You fed us,
And in prosperous times sustained us.
From the sword You saved us,
From plague You spared us,
From debilitating illness You rescued us.
Till this very moment Your compassion has accompanied us.
Your love has not forsaken us.
You will never abandon us,
Adonai our God.

עַל־כֵּן אֵבָרִים שֶׁפִּלַּגְתָּ בָּנוּ וְרוּחַ וּנְשָׁמָה שֶׁנָּפַחְתָּ בְּאַפֵּינוּ וְלָשׁוֹן אֲשֶׁר שַׂמְתָּ בְּפִינוּ. הֵן הֵם יוֹדוּ וִיבָרְכוּ וִישַׁבְּחוּ וִיפָאֲרוּ וִירוֹמְמוּ וְיַעֲרִיצוּ וְיַקְדִּישׁוּ וְיַמְלִיכוּ אֶת־שִׁמְךָ מַלְכֵּנוּ: כִּי כָל־פֶּה לְךָ יוֹדֶה. וְכָל־לָשׁוֹן לְךָ תִשָּׁבַע. וְכָל־בֶּרֶךְ לְךָ תִכְרַע. וְכָל־קוֹמָה לְפָנֶיךָ תִשְׁתַּחֲוֶה. וְכָל־לְבָבוֹת יִירָאוּךָ. וְכָל־קֶרֶב וּכְלָיוֹת יְזַמְּרוּ לִשְׁמֶךָ. כַּדָּבָר שֶׁכָּתוּב. כָּל־עַצְמוֹתַי תֹּאמַרְנָה יְיָ מִי כָמוֹךָ. מַצִּיל עָנִי מֵחָזָק מִמֶּנּוּ וְעָנִי וְאֶבְיוֹן מִגֹּזְלוֹ: מִי יִדְמֶה־לָּךְ וּמִי יִשְׁוֶה־לָּךְ וּמִי יַעֲרָךְ־לָךְ. הָאֵל הַגָּדוֹל הַגִּבּוֹר וְהַנּוֹרָא אֵל

עֶלְיוֹן קֹנֵה שָׁמַיִם וָאָרֶץ: נְהַלֶּלְךָ וּנְשַׁבֵּחֲךָ וּנְפָאֶרְךָ וּנְבָרֵךְ
אֶת־שֵׁם קָדְשֶׁךָ. כָּאָמוּר לְדָוִד בָּרְכִי נַפְשִׁי אֶת־יְיָ וְכָל־
קְרָבַי אֶת־שֵׁם קָדְשׁוֹ:

Therefore these shall sing what praise they can:
The limbs with which You have constructed us shall be our
    strings,
The tongue You have placed in us shall be the bow,
The soul You have breathed in us shall resonate the melody.
Soon with my mouth
Every mouth shall give thanks,
Every tongue shall swear its truth,
Every knee shall bow down,
Every backbone fall prostrate,
Every heart shall fill with awe,
Every inner organ sing its praise,
And the psalm verse shall come true:
"All my bones shall say, 'Incomparable is Adonai!'"

David first plucked out the chords:
"O my soul, sing praises to Adonai;
To the one
Whose Name is holy
Shout with all my inmost being!"

הָאֵל בְּתַעֲצֻמוֹת עֻזֶּךָ: הַגָּדוֹל בִּכְבוֹד שְׁמֶךָ: הַגִּבּוֹר לָנֶצַח
וְהַנּוֹרָא בְּנוֹרְאוֹתֶיךָ:

הַמֶּלֶךְ הַיּוֹשֵׁב עַל־כִּסֵּא רָם וְנִשָּׂא:

O God, whose power is firm,
O Great One, whose Name is glorious,
O Mighty One eternal, whose awesomeness is Awe itself,
O Sovereign who sits upon the high and lofty throne!

שׁוֹכֵן עַד מָרוֹם וְקָדוֹשׁ שְׁמוֹ: וְכָתוּב. רַנְּנוּ צַדִּיקִים בַּיְיָ
לַיְשָׁרִים נָאוָה תְהִלָּה: בְּפִי יְשָׁרִים תִּתְהַלָּל. וּבְדִבְרֵי
צַדִּיקִים תִּתְבָּרַךְ. וּבִלְשׁוֹן חֲסִידִים תִּתְרוֹמָם. וּבְקֶרֶב
קְדוֹשִׁים תִּתְקַדָּשׁ:

The Shechinah is our intimate forever, yet with a Name
    exalted and holy.
Sing to Adonai, those who do justly, for praise becomes the
    upright.
From the mouth of the upright comes God's praise,
Blessing is in the words of doers of justice,
Exaltation springs from the tongue of those who do more
    than is required.
From the innermost parts of holy people does God's holiness
    shine forth.

וּבְמַקְהֲלוֹת רִבְבוֹת עַמְּךָ בֵּית יִשְׂרָאֵל בְּרִנָּה יִתְפָּאַר
שִׁמְךָ מַלְכֵּנוּ בְּכָל־דּוֹר וָדוֹר: שֶׁכֵּן חוֹבַת כָּל־הַיְצוּרִים
לְפָנֶיךָ יְיָ אֱלֹהֵינוּ וֵאלֹהֵי אֲבוֹתֵינוּ (וְאִמּוֹתֵינוּ) לְהוֹדוֹת
לְהַלֵּל לְשַׁבֵּחַ לְפָאֵר לְרוֹמֵם לְהַדֵּר לְבָרֵךְ לְעַלֵּה וּלְקַלֵּס
עַל־כָּל־דִּבְרֵי שִׁירוֹת וְתִשְׁבְּחוֹת דָּוִד בֶּן־יִשַׁי עַבְדְּךָ
מְשִׁיחֶךָ:

In all our communities,
Your people Israel's house
Will praise Your Name in song,
    In whispers of the aged, in the playfulness of children,
    In the questions of the young, in the struggles of their
        parents,
For it is the obligation of us all,
Our God and God of all our generations,
To thank and sing hallel, to praise, glorify, and exalt,
To honor, bless, magnify and extol
In excess of all the words of David's songs,
All the praises penned by Jesse's son, Your servant,
Anointed to bring Your rule to earth.

YISHTABACH: The Climax of Hallel

יִשְׁתַּבַּח שִׁמְךָ לָעַד מַלְכֵּנוּ הָאֵל הַמֶּלֶךְ הַגָּדוֹל וְהַקָּדוֹשׁ
בַּשָּׁמַיִם וּבָאָרֶץ: כִּי־לְךָ נָאֶה יְיָ אֱלֹהֵינוּ וֵאלֹהֵי אֲבוֹתֵינוּ
(וְאִמּוֹתֵינוּ) שִׁיר וּשְׁבָחָה הַלֵּל וְזִמְרָה עֹז וּמֶמְשָׁלָה נֶצַח
גְּדֻלָּה וּגְבוּרָה תְּהִלָּה וְתִפְאֶרֶת קְדֻשָּׁה וּמַלְכוּת בְּרָכוֹת

וְהוֹדָאוֹת מֵעַתָּה וְעַד־עוֹלָם: בָּרוּךְ אַתָּה יְיָ אֵל מֶלֶךְ גָּדוֹל בַּתִּשְׁבָּחוֹת. אֵל הַהוֹדָאוֹת. אֲדוֹן הַנִּפְלָאוֹת. הַבּוֹחֵר בְּשִׁירֵי זִמְרָה. מֶלֶךְ אֵל חֵי הָעוֹלָמִים:

Yish-ta-bach shim-cha la-ad mal-kei-nu, ha-El ha-me-
lech ha-ga-dol ve-ha-ka-dosh ba-sha-ma-yim u-va-a-
retz. Ki le-cha na-eh, A-do-nai E-lo-hei-nu vE-lo-hei
a-vo-tei-nu (ve-i-mo-tei-nu), shir u-she-va-cha ha-llel
ve-zim-ra oz u-mem-sha-la ne-tzach ge-du-la u-ge-vu-ra
te-hi-la ve-tif-e-ret ke-du-sha u-mal-chut, be-ra-chot
ve-ho-da-ot mei-a-ta ve-ad o-lam. Ba-ruch a-ta A-do-nai
El me-lech ga-dol ba-tish-ba-chot, El ha-ho-da-ot, a-don
ha-nif-la-ot, ha-bo-cher be-shi-rei zim-ra, me-lech El chei
ha-o-la-mim.

May Your Name be praised forever, our Sovereign,
Majestic God,
Great and holy in heaven and on earth.
How fitting it is,
Adonai our God, God of our fathers and mothers,
To offer You praise and song,
Hallel and harmony,
Celebrations of Your strength and Your rule,
Your victory and greatness,
Might and power,
Honor and glory,
Holiness and majesty—
Blessings and thanks now and forever!

You are praised, Adonai,
Majestic God,
Great in praises
God of thanksgivings
Source of wonder
Guarantor of life eternal,
Who has chosen the verses of these our songs.

THE FIFTH CUP: Second Part

(Those who wish to drink a fifth cup of wine [the one poured earlier or the Cup of Elijah] do so, if they follow the Maharal of Prague's custom, without a blessing, since the authority of this custom, like washing before Karpas, is not universally recognized. One or more of the following readings may be used instead, reflecting aspects of the Fifth Cup's celebration of the ultimate fulfillment of all God's promises:)

Once a teacher drew a picture of a box. Then another picture, this time of a roof. Then of someone saying the word "Ah." Then of a toe. Another person saying the word "Ah." A door. Drums making noise. Someone saying, "Hello." A stack of hay. A nude figure.

From these pictures the teacher taught a retarded man who was unable to read how to recite the blessings for his bar mitzvah.

The pictures spell, "Ba-ruch a-to A-do-noi Elo-hay-nu . . ."
Of course.

* * * * *

It shall come to pass in the latter days
That the mountain of the house of God
Shall be established as the highest of the mountains,
And shall be raised above the hills;
And all the nations shall flow to it,
And many peoples shall come and say,
Come, let us go up to the mountain of God,
To the house of the God of Jacob;
That You may teach us Your ways
And we may walk in Your paths.
For out of Zion shall go forth Torah,
And the word of God from Jerusalem.
You will judge between the nations,
And shall decide for many peoples;
And they shall beat their swords into plowshares,
And their spears into pruning hooks;

Nation shall not lift up sword against nation,
Neither shall they learn war any more.

(Isaiah 2:1–4)

(*Lo yi-sa goy*, the Hebrew setting of this text, might be sung here [see page 147].)

DIRECTIONS: Drink from the Fifth Cup, *Ve-he-vei-ti,* "And I will bring you to the Land," in a mood of fervent hope.

(Continue with the concluding blessing below.)

THE FOURTH CUP: Belonging to God

Reflections

The Fourth Cup celebrates *Ve-la-kach-ti*, "I will take you to Me for a people, and I will become God for you" (Exodus 6:7). In this cup we may see expressed the hope for spiritual redemption, for the fulfillment of our longing to be close to God. The more we act like God's people, this fourth promise suggests, the more we can experience the Eternal One becoming God for each of us.

Let us raise our cups and celebrate that promise with the following words:

בָּרוּךְ אַתָּה יְיָ אֱלֹהֵינוּ מֶלֶךְ הָעוֹלָם. בּוֹרֵא פְּרִי הַגָּפֶן:

Ba-ruch a-ta A-do-nai E-lo-hei-nu me-lech ha-o-lam,
bo-rei pe-ri ha-ga-fen.

Praised are You, Adonai our God, Monarch over time and space, Creator of this fruit of the vine.

DIRECTIONS: Drink from the Fourth Cup, *Ve-la-kach-ti,* "I will take you," while reclining to the left, tasting the holy joy of God's presence.

CONCLUDING BLESSING

(*The concluding cup of nourishment is followed by a condensation of the Birkat Ha-Mazon, which becomes the final blessing of the Seder.*)

בָּרוּךְ אַתָּה יְיָ אֱלֹהֵינוּ מֶלֶךְ הָעוֹלָם. עַל־הַגֶּפֶן וְעַל־פְּרִי
הַגֶּפֶן. וְעַל תְּנוּבַת הַשָּׂדֶה וְעַל־אֶרֶץ חֶמְדָּה טוֹבָה

וּרְחָבָה שֶׁרָצִיתָ וְהִנְחַלְתָּ לַאֲבוֹתֵינוּ (וּלְאִמּוֹתֵינוּ) לֶאֱכוֹל
מִפִּרְיָהּ וְלִשְׂבּוֹעַ מִטּוּבָהּ: רַחֵם יְיָ אֱלֹהֵינוּ עַל־יִשְׂרָאֵל
עַמֶּךָ וְעַל־יְרוּשָׁלַיִם עִירֶךָ. וְעַל־צִיּוֹן מִשְׁכַּן כְּבוֹדֶךָ. וְעַל־
מִזְבַּחֶךָ וְעַל־הֵיכָלֶךָ. וּבְנֵה יְרוּשָׁלַיִם עִיר הַקֹּדֶשׁ בִּמְהֵרָה
בְיָמֵינוּ. וְהַעֲלֵנוּ לְתוֹכָהּ וְשַׂמְּחֵנוּ בְּבִנְיָנָהּ. וְנֹאכַל מִפִּרְיָהּ
וְנִשְׂבַּע מִטּוּבָהּ. וּנְבָרֶכְךָ עָלֶיהָ בִּקְדֻשָׁה וּבְטָהֳרָה: [וּרְצֵה
וְהַחֲלִיצֵנוּ בְּיוֹם הַשַּׁבָּת הַזֶּה] וְשַׂמְּחֵנוּ בְּיוֹם חַג הַמַּצּוֹת
הַזֶּה. כִּי־אַתָּה יְיָ טוֹב וּמֵטִיב לַכֹּל וְנוֹדֶה לְךָ עַל הָאָרֶץ
וְעַל פְּרִי הַגָּפֶן:

Thank You, Adonai our God, majesty of the universe, for the
vine and the fruit of the vine, which has flowed abundantly
this night in celebration of Your holy presence in the
redemption of our people.

Thank You for the produce of the field, the grain which has
given us matzah, through which we have tasted both our
people's suffering and their liberation.

Thank You for that sweet land, so fruitful, good, and broad,
the goal of our ancestors' trek from narrow Mitzrayim, a
bequest of love from You.

Shed compassion, Adonai our God, upon Israel Your people
and Jerusalem Your city; upon Zion, the place where we
shall most intimately encounter Your glory; and upon every
place where offerings are brought before You.

O build Jerusalem, speedily in our time, into a city worthy of
Your holiness, and bring us up into its innermost parts
jubilant in its reconstruction, nourished from its fruits, filled
with its goodness, eager to praise You for the purity of its
holiness.

[On Shabbat: Favor us with rest on this Shabbat, and]
Let us know joy on this day of the Matzah Festival, for You,
Adonai, are good, and You do good for all, and so we thank
You for the land and for the fruit of the vine.

בָּרוּךְ אַתָּה יְיָ עַל הָאָרֶץ וְעַל פְּרִי הַגָּפֶן:

Ba-ruch a-ta A-do-nai, al ha-a-retz ve-al pe-ri ha-ga-fen.

You are praised, Adonai, for the land and for the fruit of the vine.

נִרְצָה

NIRTZAH

This Feast Conclude

Farewell by the Song

לְכָה דוֹדִי נֵצֵא הַשָּׂדֶה נָלִינָה בַּכְּפָרִים: נַשְׁכִּימָה
לַכְּרָמִים נִרְאֶה אִם־פָּרְחָה הַגֶּפֶן פִּתַּח הַסְּמָדַר הֵנֵצוּ
הָרִמּוֹנִים שָׁם אֶתֵּן אֶת־דֹּדַי לָךְ: בְּרַח דּוֹדִי וּדְמֵה־לְךָ
לִצְבִי אוֹ לְעֹפֶר הָאַיָּלִים עַל הָרֵי בְשָׂמִים:

Come my love, let us go while night remains,
To the open spaces, to the towns where our people live;
When morning comes
We will awake in vineyards.

Look: the vines are blossoming!
The flowers are opening!
There are buds on the pomegranates!

This is the place to share my love
With you.

Run away with me, my love!
How like a gazelle you are,
Swift and strong,
How like the morning star:
The promise of light
Upon the fragrant mountains.

Arise, my love,
Take wing,
And come away.

(Song of Songs 7:12–13, 8:14)

* * * * *

חֲסַל סִדּוּר פֶּסַח כְּהִלְכָתוֹ.
כְּכָל־מִשְׁפָּטוֹ וְחֻקָתוֹ:
כַּאֲשֶׁר זָכִינוּ לְסַדֵּר אוֹתוֹ.
כֵּן נִזְכֶּה לַעֲשׂוֹתוֹ:
זָךְ שׁוֹכֵן מְעוֹנָה.
קוֹמֵם קְהַל מִי מָנָה:
קָרֵב נַהֵל נִטְעֵי כַנָּה.
פְּדוּיִם לְצִיּוֹן בְּרִנָּה:

Cha-sal si-dur Pe-sach ke-hil-cha-to,
Ke-chol mish-pa-to ve-chu-ka-to.
Ka-a-sher za-chi-nu le-sa-der o-to,
Ken niz-keh la-a-so-to.
Zach sho-chen me-o-nah,
Ko-mem ke-hal mi ma-nah.
Ka-rev na-hel nit-ei cha-nah,
Pe-du-yim le-Tzi-yon be-ri-nah!

The Pesach Seder, in proper form, is done,
Faithful to its laws and customs, one by one;
As the privilege of observing it tonight we've won,
May we be privileged again when a year is done.

May the Pure One who dwells above incline
To raise us up as numerous as the stars that shine,
Guiding us, plantings of Your fruitful vine,
Redeemed and singing into Zion's shrine!

לַשָׁנָה הַבָּאָה בִּירוּשָׁלָיִם:

La-sha-na ha-ba-ah bi-ru-sha-la-yim!

Next year in Jerusalem!

Next year may all humanity be redeemed!

*　　*　　*　　*　　*

BEYOND THE CONCLUSION: Counting the Omer

(This section is omitted on the first night of Pesach.)

Reflections

Freedom from slavery is not the end of our redemption, but the beginning. The encounter with God at the Reed Sea was but the prelude to the encounter at Sinai. When this week is done, the matzah of slavery and freedom will disappear, but the wine of holiness will reappear, not only on Shabbat, but at Shavuot, the conclusion of the seven weeks we begin to count on the second night of Pesach.

On the second day out of Egypt, our ancestors took a small measure, an *omer*, of barley, representing perhaps the small degree of holiness they had acquired since emerging from slavery the day before. From then until Shavuot they counted the days. . . .

Some say that every day they looked back on the progress they had made since that first full day and that first small measure; others say they relished each day for its own sake, its own growth, as days grew into a week and one week grew into seven.

How have we grown, what have we learned, this Seder night? As we begin to count the days till Revelation, let us begin to celebrate our small measures of religious progress as well.

*   *   *   *   *

The Kabbalists tell us that each of the seven weeks we count from Pesach till Shavuot—the day which marks Israel's receiving of the Torah—corresponds to one of the seven lower sefirot, the qualities of God's nature that the mystics believed govern all life. Each of these qualities, each sefirah, is shared by a major figure in the Jewish past.

Thus in the first week we emulate Abraham, with his quality of *chesed*, lovingkindness; in the second week, Isaac, of strong character, *gevurah*; in the third week, Jacob, and his appreciation of *hod*, God's glory; in the fourth week, Moses and *netzach*, eternity, reflecting the eternity of the Torah he transmitted to us; in the fifth week, Aaron and *tiferet*, the splendor of the Creation to which he strove so hard to bring peace; in the sixth week, Joseph and *yesod*, fundamental morality; in the seventh week, David and sovereignty, *malchut* and the realm of the Shechinah, the closest realm to ours, in which all life is seen as an aspect of God's rule.

From this night on, we might devote each of the weeks till Shavuot to the pursuit of that week's virtue, strengthening it in ourselves and then combining it with the virtues of the weeks preceding. In this way we can attempt to emulate our ancestors' preparations for the fiftieth day, when each of us will receive the portion destined for us in that totality of truth and virtue which is the Torah.

* * * * *

All Say Together:

בָּרוּךְ אַתָּה יְיָ אֱלֹהֵינוּ מֶלֶךְ הָעוֹלָם אֲשֶׁר קִדְּשָׁנוּ בְּמִצְוֹתָיו וְצִוָּנוּ עַל סְפִירַת הָעֹמֶר:

Ba-ruch a-ta A-do-nai E-lo-hei-nu me-lech ha-o-lam, a-sher ki-de-sha-nu be-mitz-vo-tav ve-tzi-va-nu al se-fi-rat ha-o-mer.

You are praised, Adonai our God, Monarch over time and space, who shares Your holiness with us through Your mitzvot, and now bestows on us the mitzvah of counting the omer.

On the Second Night of Pesach Say:

הַיּוֹם יוֹם אֶחָד לָעֹמֶר:

Ha-yom yom e-chad la-o-mer.

This day is Day One of the Omer.

On the Third Night of Pesach Say:

הַיּוֹם שְׁנֵי יָמִים לָעֹמֶר.

Ha-yom shnei ya-mim la-o-mer.

This day is two days of the Omer.

On the Fourth Night of Pesach Say:

הַיּוֹם שְׁלֹשָׁה יָמִים לָעֹמֶר.

Ha-yom she-lo-sha ya-mim la-o-mer.

This day is three days of the Omer.

On the Fifth Night of Pesach Say:

הַיּוֹם אַרְבָּעָה יָמִים לָעֹמֶר.

Ha-yom ar-ba-a ya-mim la-o-mer.

This day is four days of the Omer.

On the Sixth Night of Pesach Say:

הַיּוֹם חֲמִשָּׁה יָמִים לָעֹמֶר.

Ha-yom cha-mi-sha ya-mim la-o-mer.

This day is five days of the Omer.

On the Seventh Night of Pesach Say:

הַיּוֹם שִׁשָּׁה יָמִים לָעֹמֶר.

Ha-yom shi-sha ya-mim la-o-mer.

This day is six days of the Omer.

On the Eighth Night of Pesach Say:

הַיּוֹם שִׁבְעָה יָמִים שֶׁהֵם שָׁבוּעַ אֶחָד לָעֹמֶר.

Ha-yom shiv-a ya-mim, she-hem sha-vu-a e-chad la-o-mer.

This day is seven days, which are Week One of the Omer.

TRADITIONAL SONGS

כִּי לוֹ נָאֶה. כִּי לוֹ יָאֶה:

KI LO NA-EH, KI LO YA-EH: For Praise Befits You, Praise Will Ever Befit You (An Ancient Alphabetic Acrostic)

(After each set of three praises this refrain occurs: Le-cha u-le-cha ("To You and to You"), Le-cha ki le-cha ("To You, yea, to You"), Le-cha af le-cha ("To You, also to You"), Le-cha A-do-nai ha-mam-la-cha ("To You, Adonai, belongs sovereignty").

The refrain comes from the following sources:

"To You and to You": "Praise is becoming to You, O God in Zion, and to You vows are paid" (Psalm 65:2).

"To You, yea, to You": "To You, Adonai, belong grandeur and might; splendor, eternity, and glory; yea, everything in heaven and earth; sovereignty belongs to You, Adonai, who is exalted as head above all" (I Chronicles 29:11).

"To You, also to You": "To You belongs the day, also the night belongs to You" (Psalm 74:16).

"To You, Adonai, belongs sovereignty": See I Chronicles 29:11 above.

* * * * *

אַדִּיר בִּמְלוּכָה. בָּחוּר כַּהֲלָכָה. גְּדוּדָיו יֹאמְרוּ לוֹ. לְךָ
וּלְךָ. לְךָ כִּי לְךָ. לְךָ אַף לְךָ. לְךָ יְיָ הַמַּמְלָכָה. כִּי לוֹ נָאֶה.
כִּי לוֹ יָאֶה:

A-dir bim-lu-cha, ba-chur ka-ha-la-cha, ge-du-dav yom-ru lo:

Refrain: Le-cha u-le-cha, le-cha ki le-cha, le-cha af le-cha, le-cha A-do-nai ha-mam-la-cha. Ki lo na-eh, ki lo ya-eh.

Mighty in majesty, chosen by right; Your hosts say to You:

Refrain: To You and to You, To You, yea, to You, To You,
  also to You, To You, Adonai, belongs sovereignty.
For praise befits You, praise will ever befit You!

* * * * *

דָּגוּל בִּמְלוּכָה. הָדוּר כַּהֲלָכָה. וָתִיקָיו יֹאמְרוּ לוֹ. לְךָ
וּלְךָ. לְךָ כִּי לְךָ. לְךָ אַף לְךָ. לְךָ יְיָ הַמַּמְלָכָה. כִּי לוֹ נָאֶה.
כִּי לוֹ יָאֶה:

Da-gul bim-lu-cha, ha-dur ka-ha-la-cha, va-ti-kav yom-
ru lo:
    Le-cha u-le-cha . . .
    Ki lo na-eh, ki lo ya-eh.

Distinguished in sovereignty, glorious by right; Your
ancient ones say to You:
    To You and to You . . .
For Praise befits You, praise will ever befit You!

* * * * *

זַכַּאי בִּמְלוּכָה. חָסִין כַּהֲלָכָה. טַפְסְרָיו יֹאמְרוּ לוֹ. לְךָ
וּלְךָ. לְךָ כִּי לְךָ. לְךָ אַף לְךָ. לְךָ יְיָ הַמַּמְלָכָה. כִּי לוֹ נָאֶה.
כִּי לוֹ יָאֶה:

Za-kai bim-lu-cha, cha-sin ka-ha-la-cha, taf-se-rav yom-
ru lo:
    Le-cha u-le-cha . . .
    Ki lo na-eh, ki lo ya-eh.

Just in majesty, vigorous by right; Your courtiers say to You:
    To You and to You . . .
For praise befits You, praise will ever befit You!

* * * * *

יָחִיד בִּמְלוּכָה. כַּבִּיר כַּהֲלָכָה. לִמוּדָיו יֹאמְרוּ לוֹ. לְךָ
וּלְךָ. לְךָ כִּי לְךָ. לְךָ אַף לְךָ. לְךָ יְיָ הַמַּמְלָכָה. כִּי לוֹ נָאֶה.
כִּי לוֹ יָאֶה:

Ya-chid bim-lu-cha, ka-bir ka-ha-la-cha, li-mu-dav yom-
ru lo:
   Le-cha u-le-cha . . .
   Ki lo na-eh, ki lo ya-eh.

Unique in majesty, strong by right; Your scholars say to
   You: To You and to You . . .
For praise befits You, praise will ever befit You!

* * * * *

מָרוֹם בִּמְלוּכָה. נוֹרָא כַּהֲלָכָה. סְבִיבָיו יֹאמְרוּ לוֹ. לְךָ
וּלְךָ. לְךָ כִּי לְךָ. לְךָ אַף לְךָ. לְךָ יְיָ הַמַּמְלָכָה. כִּי לוֹ נָאֶה.
כִּי לוֹ יָאֶה:

Ma-rom bim-lu-cha, no-ra ka-ha-la-cha, se-vi-vav yom-
ru lo:
   Le-cha u-le-cha . . .
   Ki lo na-eh, ki lo ya-eh.

Exalted in majesty, awesome by right; all who surround You
say to You:
   To You and to You . . .
For praise befits You, praise will ever befit You!

* * * * *

עָנִיו בִּמְלוּכָה. פּוֹדֶה כַּהֲלָכָה. צַדִּיקָיו יֹאמְרוּ לוֹ. לְךָ
וּלְךָ. לְךָ כִּי לְךָ. לְךָ אַף לְךָ. לְךָ יְיָ הַמַּמְלָכָה. כִּי לוֹ נָאֶה.
כִּי לוֹ יָאֶה:

A-nav bim-lu-cha, po-deh ka-ha-la-cha, tza-di-kav yom-
ru lo:
   Le-cha u-le-cha . . .
   Ki lo na-eh, ki lo ya-eh.

Modest in majesty, redeemer by right; Your righteous ones
say to You:
To You and to You . . .
For praise befits You, praise will ever befit You!

* * * * *

קָדוֹשׁ בִּמְלוּכָה. רַחוּם כַּהֲלָכָה. שִׁנְאַנָּיו יֹאמְרוּ לוֹ. לְךָ
וּלְךָ. לְךָ כִּי לְךָ. לְךָ אַף לְךָ. לְךָ יְיָ הַמַּמְלָכָה. כִּי לוֹ נָאֶה.
כִּי לוֹ יָאֶה:

Ka-dosh bim-lu-cha, ra-chum ka-ha-la-cha, shin-a-nav
yom-ru lo:
Le-cha u-le-cha . . .
Ki lo na-eh, ki lo ya-eh.

Holy in majesty, compassionate by right; Your myriad
angels say to You:
To You and to You . . .
For praise befits You, praise will ever befit You!

* * * * *

תַּקִּיף בִּמְלוּכָה. תּוֹמֵךְ כַּהֲלָכָה. תְּמִימָיו יֹאמְרוּ לוֹ. לְךָ
וּלְךָ. לְךָ כִּי לְךָ. לְךָ אַף לְךָ. לְךָ יְיָ הַמַּמְלָכָה. כִּי לוֹ נָאֶה.
כִּי לוֹ יָאֶה:

Ta-kif bim-lu-cha, to-mech ka-ha-la-cha, te-mi-mav
yom-ru lo:
Le-cha u-le-cha . . .
Ki lo na-eh, ki lo ya-eh.

Powerful in majesty, supporting by right; Your innocents
say to You:
To You and to You . . .
For praise befits You, praise will ever befit You!

* * * * *

אַדִּיר הוּא

ADIR HU: Mighty Are You!

(An alphabetical acrostic [from fifteenth-century Germany] like
Ki Lo Na-eh, symbolizing our attempt to encompass all God's
virtues by singing one attribute for each letter of the alphabet, the
building blocks of all our speech.)

אַדִּיר הוּא. יִבְנֶה בֵיתוֹ בְּקָרוֹב.

בִּמְהֵרָה. בִּמְהֵרָה. בְּיָמֵינוּ בְּקָרוֹב.

אֵל בְּנֵה. אֵל בְּנֵה. בְּנֵה בֵיתְךָ בְּקָרוֹב:

A-dir hu, a-dir hu.
Refrain: Yiv-neh vei-to be-ka-rov,
Bim-hei-ra, bim-hei-ra, be-ya-mei-nu be-ka-
rov.
El be-nei, El be-nei, be-nei veit-cha be-ka-rov.

Mighty are You! May You rebuild Your house soon,
Speedily, speedily, in our days, soon!
O God, rebuild, O God, rebuild, rebuild Your house soon!

בָּחוּר הוּא. גָּדוֹל הוּא. דָּגוּל הוּא. יִבְנֶה בֵיתוֹ בְּקָרוֹב.

בִּמְהֵרָה. בִּמְהֵרָה. בְּיָמֵינוּ בְּקָרוֹב.

אֵל בְּנֵה. אֵל בְּנֵה. בְּנֵה בֵיתְךָ בְּקָרוֹב:

Ba-chur hu, ga-dol hu, da-gul hu, yiv-neh . . .

Select are You, grand are You, distinguished are You, may
You rebuild . . .

הָדוּר הוּא. וָתִיק הוּא. זַכַּאי הוּא. יִבְנֶה בֵיתוֹ בְּקָרוֹב.

בִּמְהֵרָה. בִּמְהֵרָה. בְּיָמֵינוּ בְּקָרוֹב.

אֵל בְּנֵה. אֵל בְּנֵה. בְּנֵה בֵיתְךָ בְּקָרוֹב:

Ha-dur hu, va-tik hu, za-kai hu, yiv-neh . . .

Glorious are You, ancient are You, just are You, may You
rebuild . . .

חָסִיד הוּא. טָהוֹר הוּא. יָחִיד הוּא. יִבְנֶה בֵיתוֹ בְּקָרוֹב.
בִּמְהֵרָה. בִּמְהֵרָה. בְּיָמֵינוּ בְּקָרוֹב.
אֵל בְּנֵה. אֵל בְּנֵה. בְּנֵה בֵיתְךָ בְּקָרוֹב:

Cha-sid hu, ta-hor hu, ya-chid hu, yiv-neh . . .

Pious are You, unstained are You, unique are You, may You rebuild . . .

כַּבִּיר הוּא. לָמוּד הוּא. מֶלֶךְ הוּא. יִבְנֶה בֵיתוֹ בְּקָרוֹב.
בִּמְהֵרָה. בִּמְהֵרָה. בְּיָמֵינוּ בְּקָרוֹב.
אֵל בְּנֵה. אֵל בְּנֵה. בְּנֵה בֵיתְךָ בְּקָרוֹב:

Ka-bir hu, la-mud hu, me-lech hu, yiv-neh . . .

Strong are You, wise are You, sovereign are You, may You rebuild . . .

נוֹרָא הוּא. סַגִּיב הוּא. עִזּוּז הוּא. יִבְנֶה בֵיתוֹ בְּקָרוֹב.
בִּמְהֵרָה. בִּמְהֵרָה. בְּיָמֵינוּ בְּקָרוֹב.
אֵל בְּנֵה. אֵל בְּנֵה. בְּנֵה בֵיתְךָ בְּקָרוֹב:

No-ra hu, sa-giv hu, i-zuz hu, yiv-neh . . .

Awesome are You, exalted are You, powerful are You, may You rebuild . . .

פּוֹדֶה הוּא. צַדִּיק הוּא. קָדוֹשׁ הוּא. יִבְנֶה בֵיתוֹ בְּקָרוֹב.
בִּמְהֵרָה. בִּמְהֵרָה. בְּיָמֵינוּ בְּקָרוֹב.
אֵל בְּנֵה. אֵל בְּנֵה. בְּנֵה בֵיתְךָ בְּקָרוֹב:

Po-deh hu, tza-dik hu, ka-dosh hu, yiv-neh . . .

Redeemer are You, righteous are You, holy are You, may You rebuild . . .

רַחוּם הוּא. שַׁדַּי הוּא. תַּקִּיף הוּא. יִבְנֶה בֵיתוֹ בְּקָרוֹב.
בִּמְהֵרָה. בִּמְהֵרָה. בְּיָמֵינוּ בְּקָרוֹב.
אֵל בְּנֵה. אֵל בְּנֵה. בְּנֵה בֵיתְךָ בְּקָרוֹב:

Ra-chum hu, sha-dai hu, ta-kif hu, yiv-neh . . .

Compassionate are you, Almighty are You, powerful are
You, may You rebuild . . .

* * * * *

אֶחָד מִי יוֹדֵעַ

ECHAD MI YO-DE-A: Who Knows One?

(Questions and answers reappear in this fifteenth- or sixteenth-
century song which plays not on the alphabet but on the numbers
1 to 13. Some people try to sing each verse in one breath!)

אֶחָד מִי יוֹדֵעַ. אֶחָד אֲנִי יוֹדֵעַ. אֶחָד אֱלֹהֵינוּ שֶׁבַּשָּׁמַיִם
וּבָאָרֶץ:

E-chad mi yo-de-a? E-chad a-ni yo-de-a:
E-chad E-lo-hei-nu she-ba-sha-ma-yim u-va-a-retz.

Who knows One? I know One! One is our God in heaven
and on earth.

שְׁנַיִם מִי יוֹדֵעַ. שְׁנַיִם אֲנִי יוֹדֵעַ. שְׁנֵי לֻחוֹת הַבְּרִית. אֶחָד
אֱלֹהֵינוּ שֶׁבַּשָּׁמַיִם וּבָאָרֶץ:

Shna-yim mi yo-de-a? Shna-yim a-ni yo-de-a:
Shnei lu-chot ha-brit, e-chad E-lo-hei-nu she-ba-sha-ma-
yim u-va-a-retz.

Who knows Two? I know Two! Two are the tablets of the
covenant, one is our God in heaven and on earth.

שְׁלֹשָׁה מִי יוֹדֵעַ. שְׁלֹשָׁה אֲנִי יוֹדֵעַ. שְׁלֹשָׁה אָבוֹת. שְׁנֵי
לֻחוֹת הַבְּרִית. אֶחָד אֱלֹהֵינוּ שֶׁבַּשָּׁמַיִם וּבָאָרֶץ:

Shlo-sha mi yo-de-a? Shlo-sha a-ni yo-de-a:
Shlo-sha a-vot, shnei lu-chot ha-brit, e-chad E-lo-hei-nu
she-ba-sha-ma-yim u-va-a-retz.

Who knows Three? I know Three! Three are the patriarchs,
two are the tablets of the covenant, one is our God in
heaven and on earth.

אַרְבַּע מִי יוֹדֵעַ. אַרְבַּע אֲנִי יוֹדֵעַ. אַרְבַּע אִמָּהוֹת. שְׁלשָׁה
אָבוֹת. שְׁנֵי לֻחוֹת הַבְּרִית. אֶחָד אֱלֹהֵינוּ שֶׁבַּשָּׁמַיִם
וּבָאָרֶץ:

Ar-ba mi yo-de-a? Ar-ba a-ni yo-de-a:
Ar-ba i-ma-hot, shlo-sha a-vot, shnei lu-chot ha-brit,
e-chad E-lo-hei-nu she-ba-sha-ma-yim u-va-a-retz.

Who knows Four? I know Four! Four are the matriarchs,
three are the patriarchs, two are the tablets of the
covenant, one is our God in heaven and on earth.

חֲמִשָּׁה מִי יוֹדֵעַ. חֲמִשָּׁה אֲנִי יוֹדֵעַ. חֲמִשָּׁה חֻמְשֵׁי תוֹרָה.
אַרְבַּע אִמָּהוֹת. שְׁלשָׁה אָבוֹת. שְׁנֵי לֻחוֹת הַבְּרִית. אֶחָד
אֱלֹהֵינוּ שֶׁבַּשָּׁמַיִם וּבָאָרֶץ:

Cha-mi-sha mi yo-de-a? Cha-mi-sha a-ni yo-de-a:
Cha-mi-sha chum-shei To-rah, ar-ba i-ma-hot, shlo-sha
a-vot, shnei lu-chot ha-brit, e-chad E-lo-hei-nu she-ba-
sha-ma-yim u-va-a-retz.

Who knows Five? I know Five! Five are the books of the
Torah, four are the matriarchs, three are the patriarchs,
two are the tablets of the covenant, one is our God in
heaven and on earth.

שִׁשָּׁה מִי יוֹדֵעַ. שִׁשָּׁה אֲנִי יוֹדֵעַ. שִׁשָּׁה סִדְרֵי מִשְׁנָה.
חֲמִשָּׁה חֻמְשֵׁי תוֹרָה. אַרְבַּע אִמָּהוֹת. שְׁלשָׁה אָבוֹת. שְׁנֵי
לֻחוֹת הַבְּרִית. אֶחָד אֱלֹהֵינוּ שֶׁבַּשָּׁמַיִם וּבָאָרֶץ:

Shi-sha mi yo-de-a? Shi-sha a-ni yo-de-a:
Shi-sha sid-rei Mish-na, cha-mi-sha chum-shei To-rah,
ar-ba i-ma-hot, shlo-sha a-vot, shnei lu-chot ha-brit,
e-chad E-lo-hei-nu she-ba-sha-ma-yim u-va-a-retz.

Who knows six? I know Six! Six are the orders of the Mishnah, five are the books of the Torah, four are the
matriarchs, three are the patriarchs, two are the tablets
of the covenant, one is our God in heaven and on earth.

שִׁבְעָה מִי יוֹדֵעַ. שִׁבְעָה אֲנִי יוֹדֵעַ. שִׁבְעָה יְמֵי שַׁבַּתָּא.
שִׁשָּׁה סִדְרֵי מִשְׁנָה. חֲמִשָּׁה חֻמְשֵׁי תוֹרָה. אַרְבַּע
אִמָּהוֹת. שְׁלֹשָׁה אָבוֹת. שְׁנֵי לֻחוֹת הַבְּרִית. אֶחָד אֱלֹהֵינוּ
שֶׁבַּשָּׁמַיִם וּבָאָרֶץ:

Shiv-a mi yo-de-a? Shiv-a a-ni yo-de-a:
Shiv-a ye-mei Sha-ba-ta, shi-sha sid-rei Mish-na, cha-mi-
sha chum-shei To-rah, ar-ba i-ma-hot, shlo-sha a-vot,
shnei lu-chot ha-brit, e-chad E-lo-hei-nu she-ba-sha-ma-
yim u-va-a-retz.

Who knows Seven? I know Seven! Seven are the days of the
week, six are the orders of the Mishnah, five are the
books of the Torah, four are the matriarchs, three are
the patriarchs, two are the tablets of the covenant, one
is our God in heaven and on earth.

שְׁמוֹנָה מִי יוֹדֵעַ. שְׁמוֹנָה אֲנִי יוֹדֵעַ. שְׁמוֹנָה יְמֵי מִילָה.
שִׁבְעָה יְמֵי שַׁבַּתָּא. שִׁשָּׁה סִדְרֵי מִשְׁנָה. חֲמִשָּׁה חֻמְשֵׁי
תוֹרָה. אַרְבַּע אִמָּהוֹת. שְׁלֹשָׁה אָבוֹת. שְׁנֵי לֻחוֹת
הַבְּרִית. אֶחָד אֱלֹהֵינוּ שֶׁבַּשָּׁמַיִם וּבָאָרֶץ:

She-mo-na mi yo-de-a? Shemo-na a-ni yo-de-a:
She-mo-na ye-mei mi-lah, shiv-a ye-mei Sha-ba-ta,
shi-sha sid-rei Mish-na, cha-mi-sha chum-shei To-rah,
ar-ba i-ma-hot, shlo-sha a-vot, shnei lu-chot ha-brit,
e-chad E-lo-hei-nu she-ba-sha-ma-yim u-va-a-retz.

Who knows Eight? I know Eight! Eight are the days till circumcision, seven are the days of the week, six are the orders of the Mishnah, five are the books of the Torah, four are the matriarchs, three are the patriarchs, two are the tablets of the covenant, one is our God in heaven and on earth.

תִּשְׁעָה מִי יוֹדֵעַ. תִּשְׁעָה אֲנִי יוֹדֵעַ. תִּשְׁעָה יַרְחֵי לֵדָה. שְׁמוֹנָה יְמֵי מִילָה. שִׁבְעָה יְמֵי שַׁבַּתָּא. שִׁשָּׁה סִדְרֵי מִשְׁנָה. חֲמִשָּׁה חֻמְשֵׁי תוֹרָה. אַרְבַּע אִמָּהוֹת. שְׁלֹשָׁה אָבוֹת. שְׁנֵי לֻחוֹת הַבְּרִית. אֶחָד אֱלֹהֵינוּ שֶׁבַּשָּׁמַיִם וּבָאָרֶץ:

Tish-a mi yo-de-a? Tish-a a-ni yo-de-a:
Tish-a yar-chei lei-da, shemo-na ye-mei mi-lah, shiv-a ye-mei Sha-ba-ta, shi-sha sid-rei Mish-na, cha-mi-sha chum-shei To-rah, ar-ba i-ma-hot, shlo-sha a-vot, shnei lu-chot ha-brit, e-chad E-lo-hei-nu she-ba-sha-ma-yim u-va-a-retz.

Who knows Nine? I know Nine! Nine are the months to childbirth, eight are the days to circumcision, seven are the days of the week, six are the orders of the Mishnah, five are the books of the Torah, four are the matriarchs, three are the patriarchs, two are the tablets of the covenant, one is our God in heaven and on earth.

עֲשָׂרָה מִי יוֹדֵעַ. עֲשָׂרָה אֲנִי יוֹדֵעַ. עֲשָׂרָה דִּבְּרַיָּא. תִּשְׁעָה יַרְחֵי לֵדָה. שְׁמוֹנָה יְמֵי מִילָה. שִׁבְעָה יְמֵי שַׁבַּתָּא. שִׁשָּׁה סִדְרֵי מִשְׁנָה. חֲמִשָּׁה חֻמְשֵׁי תוֹרָה. אַרְבַּע אִמָּהוֹת. שְׁלֹשָׁה אָבוֹת. שְׁנֵי לֻחוֹת הַבְּרִית. אֶחָד אֱלֹהֵינוּ שֶׁבַּשָּׁמַיִם וּבָאָרֶץ:

A-sa-ra mi yo-de-a? A-sa-ra a-ni yo-de-a:
A-sa-ra dib-ra-ya, tish-a yar-chei lei-da, shemo-na ye-mei mi-lah, shiv-a ye-mei Sha-ba-ta, shi-sha sid-rei Mish-na, cha-mi-sha chum-shei To-rah, ar-ba i-ma-hot, shlo-sha a-vot, shnei lu-chot ha-brit, e-chad E-lo-hei-nu she-ba-sha-ma-yim u-va-a-retz.

Who knows Ten? I know Ten! Ten are the Words from Sinai, nine are the months to childbirth, eight are the days to circumcision, seven are the days of the week, six are the orders of the Mishnah, five are the books of the Torah, four are the matriarchs, three are the patriarchs, two are the tablets of the covenant, one is our God in heaven and on earth.

אַחַד עָשָׂר מִי יוֹדֵעַ. אַחַד עָשָׂר אֲנִי יוֹדֵעַ. אַחַד עָשָׂר כּוֹכְבַיָּא. עֲשָׂרָה דִבְּרַיָּא. תִּשְׁעָה יַרְחֵי לֵדָה. שְׁמוֹנָה יְמֵי מִילָה. שִׁבְעָה יְמֵי שַׁבַּתָּא. שִׁשָּׁה סִדְרֵי מִשְׁנָה. חֲמִשָּׁה חֻמְשֵׁי תוֹרָה. אַרְבַּע אִמָּהוֹת. שְׁלֹשָׁה אָבוֹת. שְׁנֵי לֻחוֹת הַבְּרִית. אֶחָד אֱלֹהֵינוּ שֶׁבַּשָּׁמַיִם וּבָאָרֶץ:

A-chad a-sar mi yo-de-a? A-chad a-sar a-ni yo-de-a:
A-chad a-sar koch-va-ya, a-sa-ra dib-ra-ya, tish-a yar-chei lei-da, shemo-na ye-mei mi-lah, shiv-a ye-mei Sha-ba-ta, shi-sha sid-rei Mish-na, cha-mi-sha chum-shei To-rah, ar-ba i-ma-hot, shlo-sha a-vot, shnei lu-chot ha-brit, e-chad E-lo-hei-nu she-ba-sha-ma-yim u-va-a-retz.

Who knows Eleven? I know Eleven! Eleven are the stars in Joseph's dream, ten are the Words from Sinai, nine are the months to childbirth, eight are the days to circumcision, seven are the days of the week, six are the orders of the Mishnah, five are the books of the Torah, four are the matriarchs, three are the patriarchs, two are the tablets of the covenant, one is our God in heaven and on earth.

שְׁנֵים עָשָׂר מִי יוֹדֵעַ. שְׁנֵים עָשָׂר אֲנִי יוֹדֵעַ. שְׁנֵים עָשָׂר שִׁבְטַיָּא. אַחַד עָשָׂר כּוֹכְבַיָּא. עֲשָׂרָה דִבְּרַיָּא. תִּשְׁעָה יַרְחֵי לֵדָה. שְׁמוֹנָה יְמֵי מִילָה. שִׁבְעָה יְמֵי שַׁבַּתָּא. שִׁשָּׁה סִדְרֵי מִשְׁנָה. חֲמִשָּׁה חֻמְשֵׁי תוֹרָה. אַרְבַּע אִמָּהוֹת. שְׁלֹשָׁה אָבוֹת. שְׁנֵי לֻחוֹת הַבְּרִית. אֶחָד אֱלֹהֵינוּ שֶׁבַּשָּׁמַיִם וּבָאָרֶץ:

Shneim a-sar mi yo-de-a? Shneim a-sar a-ni yo-de-a:
Shneim a-sar shiv-ta-ya, a-chad a-sar koch-va-ya, a-sa-ra
dib-ra-ya, tish-a yar-chei lei-da, shemo-na ye-mei mi-lah,
shiv-a ye-mei Sha-ba-ta, shi-sha sid-rei Mish-na, cha-mi-
sha chum-shei To-rah, ar-ba i-ma-hot, shlo-sha a-vot,
shnei lu-chot ha-brit, e-chad E-lo-hei-nu she-ba-sha-ma-
yim u-va-a-retz.

Who knows Twelve? I know Twelve! Twelve are the tribes,
eleven are the stars in Joseph's dream, ten are the
Words from Sinai, nine are the months to childbirth,
eight are the days to circumcision, seven are the days of
the week, six are the orders of the Mishnah, five are the
books of the Torah, four are the matriarchs, three are
the patriarchs, two are the tablets of the covenant, one
is our God in heaven and on earth.

שְׁלֹשָׁה עָשָׂר מִי יוֹדֵעַ. שְׁלֹשָׁה עָשָׂר אֲנִי יוֹדֵעַ. שְׁלֹשָׁה
עָשָׂר מִדַּיָּא. שְׁנֵים עָשָׂר שִׁבְטַיָּא. אַחַד עָשָׂר כּוֹכְבַיָּא.
עֲשָׂרָה דִבְּרַיָּא. תִּשְׁעָה יַרְחֵי לֵדָה. שְׁמוֹנָה יְמֵי מִילָה.
שִׁבְעָה יְמֵי שַׁבַּתָּא. שִׁשָּׁה סִדְרֵי מִשְׁנָה. חֲמִשָּׁה חֻמְשֵׁי
תוֹרָה. אַרְבַּע אִמָּהוֹת. שְׁלֹשָׁה אָבוֹת. שְׁנֵי לֻחוֹת
הַבְּרִית. אֶחָד אֱלֹהֵינוּ שֶׁבַּשָּׁמַיִם וּבָאָרֶץ:

Shlo-sha a-sar mi yo-de-a? Shlo-sha a-sar a-ni yo-de-a:
Shlo-sha a-sar mi-da-ya, shneim a-sar shiv-ta-ya, a-chad
a-sar koch-va-ya, a-sa-ra dib-ra-ya, shemo-na ye-mei
mi-lah, shiv-a ye-mei Sha-ba-ta, shi-sha sid-rei Mish-na,
cha-mi-sha chum-shei To-rah, ar-ba i-ma-hot, shlo-sha
a-vot, shnei lu-chot ha-brit, e-chad E-lo-hei-nu she-ba-
sha-ma-yim u-va-a-retz.

Who knows Thirteen? I know Thirteen. Thirteen are God's
Qualities, twelve are the tribes, eleven are the stars in
Joseph's dream, ten are the Words from Sinai, nine are
the months to childbirth, eight are the days to circumcision, seven are the days of the week, six are the orders
of the Mishnah, five are the books of the Torah, four
are the matriarchs, three are the patriarchs, two are the
tablets of the covenant, one is our God in heaven and
on earth!

חַד גַּדְיָא

CHAD GAD-YA: An Only Kid

(Allegorical understandings abound for this beloved song, which may date from as early as the thirteenth century. Perhaps it is the story of Israel, acquired by God through the two tablets of the covenant [two zuzim], and subsequently subjected to the persecutions of those cats from Assyria, dogged Babylonia, cudgel-wielding Persia, the fiery Macedonians led by Alexander, the floodwaters of Rome, the ox-like Saracens, the slaughtering Crusaders, and the Angel of Death—all of whom will ultimately be overcome by the Blessed Holy One. [Take note, tyrants of our own time!]

Perhaps the song is a promise of victory not only over external oppressors but also over those inner enemies that eat away at our souls. Ultimately those too, and death as well, will be overcome by the Holy One, and the eternal life denied us in Eden will be restored to us all. What an uplifting thought, worthy of this rousing melody, on which to bring the Seder to a close!)

חַד גַּדְיָא חַד גַּדְיָא דְּזַבִּן אַבָּא בִּתְרֵי זוּזֵי.
חַד גַּדְיָא חַד גַּדְיָא:

Chad gad-ya, chad gad-ya, de-za-bin a-ba bit-rei zu-zei,
Chad gad-ya, chad gad-ya.

An only kid, an only kid, my father bought for two zuzim,
Chad gad-ya, chad gad-ya (An only kid, an only kid).

וְאָתָא שׁוּנְרָא. וְאָכְלָה לְגַדְיָא. דְּזַבִּן אַבָּא בִּתְרֵי זוּזֵי.
חַד גַּדְיָא חַד גַּדְיָא:

Ve-a-ta shun-ra ve-ach-la le-gad-ya, de-za-bin a-ba bit-
rei zu-zei,
Chad gad-ya, chad gad-ya.

Then came the cat and ate the kid my father bought for
two zuzim,
Chad gad-ya, chad gad-ya (An only kid, an only kid).

וְאָתָא כַלְבָּא. וְנָשַׁךְ לְשׁוּנְרָא. דְּאָכְלָה לְגַדְיָא. דְּזַבִּן אַבָּא
בִּתְרֵי זוּזֵי.
חַד גַּדְיָא חַד גַּדְיָא:

Ve-a-ta chal-ba ve-na-shach le-shun-ra de-ach-lah le-
gad-ya,
De-za-bin a-ba bit-rei zu-zei, chad gad-ya, chad gad-ya.

Then came the dog and bit the cat that ate the kid my
father bought for two zuzim,
Chad gad-ya, chad gad-ya (An only kid, an only kid).

וְאָתָא חוּטְרָא. וְהִכָּה לְכַלְבָּא דְּנָשַׁךְ לְשׁוּנְרָא דְּאָכְלָה
לְגַדְיָא. דְּזַבִּן אַבָּא בִּתְרֵי זוּזֵי.
חַד גַּדְיָא חַד גַּדְיָא:

Ve-a-ta chut-ra ve-hi-ka le-chal-ba de-na-shach le-
shun-ra de-ach-la le-gad-ya,
De-za-bin a-ba bit-rei zu-zei, chad gad-ya, chad gad-ya.

Then came the stick and beat the dog that bit the cat
that ate the kid my father bought for two zuzim,
Chad gad-ya, chad gad-ya (An only kid, an only kid).

וְאָתָא נוּרָא. וְשָׂרַף לְחוּטְרָא. דְּהִכָּה לְכַלְבָּא. דְּנָשַׁךְ
לְשׁוּנְרָא. דְּאָכְלָה לְגַדְיָא. דְּזַבִּן אַבָּא בִּתְרֵי זוּזֵי.
חַד גַּדְיָא חַד גַּדְיָא:

Ve-a-ta nu-ra ve-sa-raf le-chut-ra de-hi-ka le-chal-ba
de-na-shach le-shun-ra de-ach-la le-gad-ya,
De-za-bin a-ba bit-rei zu-zei, chad gad-ya, chad gad-ya.

Then came the fire and burnt the stick that beat the dog
that bit the cat that ate the kid my father bought for two
zuzim,
Chad gad-ya, chad gad-ya (An only kid, an only kid).

וְאָתָא מַיָּא. וְכָבָה לְנוּרָא. דְּשָׂרַף לְחוּטְרָא. דְּהִכָּה
לְכַלְבָּא. דְּנָשַׁךְ לְשׁוּנְרָא. דְּאָכְלָה לְגַדְיָא. דְּזַבִּן אַבָּא
בִּתְרֵי זוּזֵי.
חַד גַּדְיָא חַד גַּדְיָא:

Ve-a-ta ma-ya ve-cha-va le-nu-ra de-sa-raf le-chut-ra
de-hi-ka le-chal-ba de-na-shach le-shun-ra de-ach-la le-
gad-ya,
De-za-bin a-ba bit-rei zu-zei, chad gad-ya, chad gad-ya.

Then came the water and quenched the fire that burnt
the stick that beat the dog that bit the cat that ate the
kid my father bought for two zuzim,
Chad gad-ya, chad gad-ya (An only kid, an only kid).

וְאָתָא תוֹרָא. וְשָׁתָא לְמַיָּא. דְּכָבָה לְנוּרָא. דְּשָׂרַף
לְחוּטְרָא. דְּהִכָּה לְכַלְבָּא. דְּנָשַׁךְ לְשׁוּנְרָא. דְּאָכְלָה
לְגַדְיָא. דְּזַבִּן אַבָּא בִּתְרֵי זוּזֵי.
חַד גַּדְיָא חַד גַּדְיָא:

Ve-a-ta to-ra ve-sha-ta le-ma-ya de-cha-va le-nu-ra de-
sa-raf le-chut-ra de-hi-ka le-chal-ba de-na-shach le-
shun-ra de-ach-la le-gad-ya,
De-za-bin a-ba bit-rei zu-zei, chad gad-ya, chad gad-ya.

Then came the ox and drank the water that quenched the fire that burnt the stick that beat the dog that bit the cat that ate the kid my father bought for two zuzim, *Chad gad-ya, chad gad-ya* (An only kid, an only kid).

וְאָתָא הַשּׁוֹחֵט. וְשָׁחַט לְתוֹרָא. דְּשָׁתָא לְמַיָּא. דְּכָבָה
לְנוּרָא. דְּשָׂרַף לְחוּטְרָא. דְּהִכָּה לְכַלְבָּא דְּנָשַׁךְ לְשׁוּנְרָא.
דְּאָכְלָה לְגַדְיָא. דְּזַבִּן אַבָּא בִּתְרֵי זוּזֵי.
חַד גַּדְיָא חַד גַּדְיָא:

Ve-a-ta ha-sho-chet ve-sha-chat le-to-ra de-sha-ta le-ma-ya de-cha-va le-nu-ra de-sa-raf le-chut-ra de-hi-ka le-chal-ba de-na-shach le-shun-ra de-ach-la le-gad-ya,
De-za-bin a-ba bit-rei zu-zei, chad gad-ya, chad gad-ya.

Then came the shochet (kosher slaughterer) and slaughtered the ox that drank the water that quenched the fire that burnt the stick that beat the dog that bit the cat that ate the kid my father bought for two zuzim, *Chad gad-ya, chad gad-ya* (An only kid, an only kid).

וְאָתָא מַלְאַךְ הַמָּוֶת. וְשָׁחַט לְשׁוֹחֵט. דְּשָׁחַט לְתוֹרָא.
דְּשָׁתָא לְמַיָּא. דְּכָבָה לְנוּרָא. דְּשָׂרַף לְחוּטְרָא. דְּהִכָּה
לְכַלְבָּא. דְּנָשַׁךְ לְשׁוּנְרָא. דְּאָכְלָה לְגַדְיָא. דְּזַבִּן אַבָּא
בִּתְרֵי זוּזֵי.
חַד גַּדְיָא חַד גַּדְיָא:

Ve-a-ta mal-ach ha-ma-vet ve-sha-chat le-sho-chet de-sha-chat le-to-ra de-sha-ta le-ma-ya de-cha-va le-nu-ra de-sa-raf le-chut-ra de-hi-ka le-chal-ba de-na-shach le-shun-ra de-ach-la le-gad-ya,
De-za-bin a-ba bit-rei zu-zei, chad gad-ya, chad gad-ya.

Then came the Angel of Death and slaughtered the shochet that slaughtered the ox that drank the water that quenched the fire that burnt the stick that beat the dog that bit the cat that ate the kid my father bought for two zuzim,
Chad gad-ya, chad gad-ya (An only kid, an only kid).

וְאָתָא הַקָּדוֹשׁ בָּרוּךְ הוּא. וְשָׁחַט לְמַלְאַךְ הַמָּוֶת. דְּשָׁחַט
לְשׁוֹחֵט. דְּשָׁחַט לְתוֹרָא. דְּשָׁתָא לְמַיָּא. דְּכָבָה לְנוּרָא.
דְּשָׂרַף לְחוּטְרָא. דְּהִכָּה לְכַלְבָּא. דְּנָשַׁךְ לְשׁוּנְרָא.
דְּאָכְלָה לְגַדְיָא. דְּזַבֵּן אַבָּא בִּתְרֵי זוּזֵי.
חַד גַּדְיָא חַד גַּדְיָא:

Ve-a-ta ha-ka-dosh ba-ruch hu ve-sha-chat le-mal-ach
ha-ma-vet de-sha-chat le-sho-chet de-sha-chat le-to-ra
de-sha-ta le-ma-ya de-cha-va le-nu-ra de-sa-raf le-
chut-ra de-hi-ka le-chal-ba de-na-shach le-shun-ra de-
ach-la le-gad-ya,
De-za-bin a-ba bit-rei zu-zei, chad gad-ya, chad gad-ya.

Then came the Blessed Holy One and slaughtered the
Angel of Death that slaughtered the shochet that
slaughtered the ox that drank the water that quenched
the fire that burned the stick that beat the dog that bit
the cat that ate the kid my father bought for two zuzim,
Chad gad-ya, chad gad-ya (An only kid, an only kid)!

* * * * *

CONTEMPORARY SONGS

U-SHE-AV-TEM MA-YIM (p. 16)

U-she-av-tem ma-yim be-sa-son

Mi-ma-ay-nei ha-ye-shu-a.

Joyfully shall you pour water
From the springs of righteous victory.

וּשְׁאַבְתֶּם מַיִם בְּשָׂשׂוֹן
מִמַּעַיְנֵי הַיְשׁוּעָה.

DO-DI LI (p. 17)

דּוֹדִי לִי וַאֲנִי לוֹ
הָרוֹעֶה בַּשׁוֹשַׁנִּים.
מִי זֹאת עוֹלָה מִן הַמִּדְבָּר
מִי זֹאת עוֹלָה
מְקֻטֶּרֶת מוֹר וּלְבוֹנָה
דּוֹדִי לִי . . .

לְבַבְתִּינִי אֲחוֹתִי כַלָּה
לְבַבְתִּינִי כַלָּה
דּוֹדִי לִי . . .
עוּרִי צָפוֹן
וּבוֹאִי תֵימָן
דּוֹדִי לִי . . .

Refrain: Do-di li va-a-ni lo
Ha-ro-eh ba-sho-sha-nim.

Mi zot o-la min ha-mid-bar
Mi zot o-la
Me-ku-te-ret mor u-le-vo-na.

Refrain

Li-bav-ti-ni a-cho-ti ka-la
Li-bav-ti-ni ka-la

Refrain

U-ri tza-fon u-vo-i tei-man
U-ri tza-fon u-vo-i tei-man

Refrain

My beloved and I belong to each other,
Feeding among the lilies.

Who is that going up from the wilderness
Burning with myrrh and frankincense?

You have ravished my heart
My sister, my bride.

Awaken, north wind,
And come, O south wind.

THE BALLAD OF THE FOUR CHILDREN
(To the tune of "My Darling Clementine") (p. 33)

Said the parents to their children, "At the Seder you will dine,
You will eat your fill of matzah, you will drink four cups of wine."

Now these parents had four children, yes their kids they numbered four,
One was wise and one was wicked, one was simple and a bore.

And the fourth was sweet and winsome, was so young and also small,
While the others asked the questions, this one could not speak at all.

Said the wise one to the parents, "Would you please explain the laws?
Of the customs of the Seder, will you please explain the cause?"

And the parents proudly answered, "Cause our forebears ate in speed,
Ate the Pesach lamb 'ere midnight, and from slavery were freed.

"So we follow their example, and 'ere midnight we must eat
The afikomon (O so tasty!) which must be our final treat."

Then did sneer the child so wicked, "What does all this mean
to you?"
And the parents' voice was bitter, as their grief and anger
grew.
"If yourself you don't consider as a child of Isra-el,
Then for you this has no meaning, you could be a slave as
well."
Then the simple child said simply, "What is this?" And
quietly,
The good parents told their offspring, "We were freed from
slavery."
But the youngest child was silent, and just could not ask at
all,
But with eyes all bright with wonder, listened to the details
all.
Now, dear children, heed the lesson, and remember ever-
more,
What the parents told their children, told their kids that
numbered four.

THE HAMMER SONG

If I had a hammer
I'd hammer in the morning
I'd hammer in the evening
All over this land.
I'd hammer out danger
I'd hammer out a warning
I'd hammer out love between
My brothers and my sisters
All over this land.

If I had a bell,
I'd ring it in the morning
I'd ring it in the evening
All over this land.
I'd ring out danger
I'd ring out a warning
I'd ring out love between
My brothers and my sisters
All over this land.

If I had a song
I'd sing it in the morning
I'd sing it in the evening
All over this land.
I'd sing out danger
I'd sing out a warning
I'd sing out love between
My brothers and my sisters
All over this land.

Well, I got a hammer
And I've got a bell
And I've got a song
All over this land.
It's the hammer of justice
It's the bell of freedom
It's the song about love between
My brothers and my sisters
All over this land.

FOLLOW THE DRINKING GOURD

(This song, from the period of Black slavery, urges Blacks escaping from
their chains to keep their eyes on the Big Dipper [the "drinking gourd"]
which would point them toward the North, toward freedom.)

Refrain: Follow the drinking gourd,
Follow the drinking gourd,
For the old man is a-waiting
For to carry you to freedom,
Follow the drinking gourd.

When the sun comes back
And the first quail calls,
Follow the drinking gourd
For the old man is a-waiting
For to carry you to freedom,
Follow the drinking gourd.
Refrain

The river ends between two hills,
Follow the drinking gourd,
There's another river on the other side,
Follow the drinking gourd.
　Refrain

The river bank will make a mighty good road,
The dead trees will show you the way
On the left foot, peg foot travelin' on,
Follow the drinking gourd.
　Refrain

LO YISSA GOY

Lo yissa goy el goy cherev
Ve-lo yil-m'du od mil-chama.

(Nation shall not lift up sword
against nation, neither shall they
study war anymore.)

לֹא־יִשָּׂא גוֹי
אֶל־גּוֹי חֶרֶב
וְלֹא־יִלְמְדוּ עוֹד
מִלְחָמָה

DOWN BY THE RIVERSIDE

Gonna lay down my sword and shield
Down by the riverside
Down by the riverside
Down by the riverside
Gonna lay down my sword and shield
Down by the riverside
I ain't gonna study war no more.

Refrain: I ain't gonna study war no more
　　　　 I ain't gonna study war no more
　　　　 I ain't gonna study war no more
　　　　 I ain't gonna study war no more
　　　　 I ain't gonna study war no more
　　　　 I ain't gonna study war no more

I'm gonna lay down that atom bomb
Down by the riverside
Down by the riverside
Down by the riverside
I'm gonna lay down that atom bomb
Down by the riverside
I ain't gonna study war no more
    Refrain

WE SHALL OVERCOME

We shall overcome, we shall overcome,
We shall overcome, someday, someday.

Refrain: Oh, deep in my heart,
        I do believe
        We shall overcome, someday.

ALLY, ALLY OXEN FREE

Time to let the rain fall
Without us to interfere
Time to let the trees grow tall
Into a sky that's clear;
Time to let our children
Live in a land that's free
Ally ally ally ally oxen free
Ally ally ally ally oxen free.

Time to blow the smoke away
And look at the sky again;
Time to let our friends know
We'd like to begin again;
Time to send the message
Across the land and sea:
Ally ally ally ally oxen free
Ally ally ally ally oxen free.

Strong and weak
Mild and meek
No more hide and seek.

Time to see the fairness
Of a children's game;
Time for grown-ups all to stop
And learn to do the same;
Time to make our minds up
That the world at last will be,
Ally ally ally ally oxen free
Ally ally ally ally oxen free.

ACKNOWLEDGMENTS

This Haggadah grew out of the B'nai Brith Hillel movement, that noble community of rabbis, social workers, educators, students, and professors who plant the seeds of Jewish life and truth in the groves of Academe, daily nurturing them and each other as they journey from the darkness into the light. This book reflects a sheaf of suggestions for each of the Seder's major sections which Hillel directors communicated to me: alternatives to long readings, an abundance of transliterations, songs, selections from the Song of Songs, and insights into the sage Hillel as he peers out here and there from the Haggadah text. This Haggadah is a flower of the Hillel movement, and I hope my colleagues and the students and faculty who will use it will be nourished by its fruit.

But Bernard Scharfstein of Ktav, who first suggested that I compile this Haggadah, intended it not only for Hillel foundations, but for all those who bring the community into their halls in public Seders and into their homes for family Seders. Bernie is filled with infectious enthusiasm, wonderfully wild ideas, and messianic dreams whose partial fulfillment he accepts with cheerful resignation, only to rise again to suggest six or seven more. He is a terrific publisher to work with.

In the International Center of Hillel I have been greatly aided by two associate international directors, Rabbi Samuel Z. Fishman, now executive director of the Jewish Campus Activities Board for Washington, D.C., and Rabbi William Rudolph. The appearance of this Haggadah coincides with the appearance of Hillel's new International Director, Richard Joel, whose personal dedication to bringing Hillel work into the light of public recognition has inspired us all.

Closer to home, I am greatly indebted to my staff at Los Angeles Hillel Council—Marge Taylor, Janice Berlin, Shirley Rosenthal, and Caty Konigsberg, for their patience and support during the completion of this project. Some of the more difficult typing was done by our secretary Sarah Kalevitch, whose speed, accuracy, and good humor are a daily delight.

Inside my own home, patience, support, and humor abound. My companion, Carol Levy, has only in recent weeks been able to reclaim our house from the spread of this manuscript, and its pages are sprinkled with insights and suggestions which reflect her wisdom. Some of the typing and paste-ups were done by our daughters, Sarah Miriam and Elizabeth Mauree, now eleven and one half, and eight respectively, who have graciously surrendered time with me to this book's demands. My family has helped me understand the gratitude of the lover in the Song of Songs who says, "I have come to the garden—my sister, my bride—gathering my fragrant spices." The four of us have planted a garden together, and our daily life is a gathering of its perpetually unfolding spice.

Home, of course, is where most people's memories of the Seder begins. Mine begin with my late grandmother, Anna Lipsky Trottenberg, and continue through Seders with our friends Phil and Meta and Joshua and Estelle Morrison, and with my late parents, where my mother Miriam would re-create my grandmother's recipes and my father Mauree and I would argue over how much we should cut from the Haggadah. (Suggestions for deletions in the Leader's Guide are a tribute to him.) My teacher and friend at the Hebrew Union College, Dr. Eugene Mihaly, has added to these memories, as have all the members of our Havurah. Since my marriage, Carol's parents Herman and Eleanor Kretzer have treated us to Seder at her uncle Dr. Leo and Betty Stoller's house. As their children—and ours—take over more and more of the Seder leadership, they bear witness to the eternality of this ancient Jewish day: four generations have inspired this Haggadah.

To all those who would create a home for loved ones and strangers looking to celebrate our flight to freedom, this book is dedicated.

* * * * *

The following publishers and authors have generously granted permission to print excerpts from the works indicated, for which we are most grateful. (R) indicates that the selection has been somewhat revised by the editor. Every effort has been made to locate copyright holders of original material. Omissions and errors will be corrected in forthcoming editions.

Harper and Row. "In physics," p. 97, reprinted from Philip P. Hallie, *Lest Innocent Blood Be Shed,* © 1979 by Philip P. Hallie. Permission granted by Harper and Row at the request of Philip P. Hallie.

* * * * *

Other acknowledgements:

To the late Ben Aronin, author of "The Ballad of the Four Children," pp. 144f., revised by Cantor William Sharlin, Rabbi Sandy Bogin, and Carol anad Elizabeth Levy.

To Rabbi Ari Cartun, Director of Hillel at Stanford University, for the Alternative Karpas, p. 18.

To Rabbi Dan Dorfman, Director of Hillel at San Francisco State University, for rendering the Four Questions as the "Four Puzzlements," p. 25.

To Tamar Fishman for the paper cut design on the title page.

To Cantor William Sharlin, for checking the sources of the Contemporary Songs.

To Rabbi Jeffrey Summit, director of Hillel at Tufts University, for his insightful critique of the manuscript.

*　*　*　*　*

Other English readings and translations, not mentioned above, are the work of the editor.